The

Reference

Shelf

Changing U.S. Demographics

Edited by Norris Smith

The Reference Shelf
Volume 74 • Number 1

The H.W. Wilson Company
2002

The Reference Shelf

The books in this series contain reprints of articles, excerpts from books, addresses on current issues, and studies of social trends in the United States and other countries. There are six separately bound numbers in each volume, all of which are usually published in the same calendar year. Numbers one through five are each devoted to a single subject, providing background information and discussion from various points of view and concluding with a subject index and comprehensive bibliography that lists books, pamphlets, and abstracts of additional articles on the subject. The final number of each volume is a collection of recent speeches, and it contains a cumulative speaker index. Books in the series may be purchased individually or on subscription.

Library of Congress has cataloged this serial title as follows:

Changing U.S. Demographics / edited by Norris Smith.
    p.cm.—(The reference shelf; v. 74, no. 1)
  Includes bibliographical references and index.
  ISBN 0-8242-1010-7
  1. United States—Census, 22nd, 2000. 2. United States—Population. I. Title: Changing U.S. demographics. II. Smith, Norris. III. Series.

HA201.12 .C49 2002
304.6'2'0973—dc21

2001056792

Visit H.W. Wilson's Web site: www.hwwilson.com

Printed in the United States of America

Contents

List of Figures

Preface

Every ten years the census arrives, like a giant surprise package that scholars, journalists, and citizens will unwrap piece by piece and pick over in amazement, as they have done ever since the Constitution was adopted in 1787. The American census is unusual in that it was originally mandated not to raise taxes or armies (as was customary in the Old World) but to assure fair political representation. Under the Constitution, states were to be represented equally in the Senate but proportionately in the House of Representatives, according to population. Thus an original census was necessary to determine the population; it was carried out in 1790,[*] and the Constitution decreed that it be repeated at 10-year intervals.

As the population grew, states acquired additional representatives, and so Congress expanded by fairly simple arithmetic until 1911, when a cap was placed upon the number of seats in the House. From then on, changes in population had to be reflected by readjusting the numbers within the grand total of 435, some states losing seats and others gaining after each population count. State representation in the Electoral College, which chooses the president, is also affected by the census, since each state is allowed as many electoral votes as it has senators and representatives combined.

Over the years the role of the census has expanded to take in additional functions. While the census still serves to determine the composition of the House of Representatives and the Electoral College, today it also influences government spending. A great deal of federal money is now allocated and distributed according to population statistics, particularly in programs designed to help first-time homebuyers, college students, veterans, the poor, minority groups, the elderly, and children. Besides direct benefits, there are grants to municipalities for roads, schools, water treatment plants, and so forth, often tied to population. Every state, indeed every town in the country has an interest here. (Rural towns have been known to lobby vigorously to acquire large state prisons, full of offenders from the city, who will skew the town's demographic profile and make it eligible for increased federal aid.)

Almost equally vital is the information the census can provide for merchants and advertisers, town planners, social service administrators, and politicians; good demographic data are essential for all sorts of plans. Whether a town would be wise to invest in a new school or some low-cost senior housing;

---

[*] It disclosed a population of 3.9 million, about as many people as now live in Puerto Rico, and was the first census ever to be made public.

whether a hospital should hire a full-time translator, whether a TV commercial should have a Latin beat—these are all decisions that prompt people to consult the census. Its figures are therefore studied avidly, both for what they say and for what they suggest about the future.

Not surprisingly, the 2000 Census was the subject of much political wrangling, both before and after Census Day (April 1). The main issue was the reliability of the data. It is extremely difficult—some would say impossible—to count all the people in the United States with perfect accuracy. The Census Bureau uses a two-pronged approach, mailing out questionnaires to every known address and then sending agents around to follow up on the questionnaires that have not been returned. (Agents bearing forms are also sent to homeless shelters, military barracks, college dormitories, and fairs and carnivals.) Most people receive the "short form," a page of questions about the number of people who reside at the address, their gender, age, ethnic group, and family relationship; however, a sizable number get the dreaded "long form," which asks further, and much more detailed, questions and serves as the basis for reports on education, employment, income, housing, household property, and health. The people most likely to be missed by these methods are those who rent short-term or have no fixed address—poor people, usually, who are living close to the margins of society. At the opposite extreme, people who are well fixed may be counted twice, because they are likely to have more than one address.

In an effort to improve upon the 1990 census, which was widely seen as having fallen short in its reach and accuracy, the Bureau launched an advertising campaign for 2000 explaining the advantages to communities of having an accurate count and reassuring people that their names and addresses would not be passed along to the IRS, the INS, or the landlord. (The Bureau shares statistics with other government agencies—that is its principal function—but personal names and addresses are separated from the forms and kept under seal for 72 years, by which time they are mostly of interest to genealogists.) The Bureau also enlisted the help of community leaders to get its message across. The census that resulted in 2000 was certainly an improvement over the previous one, especially in the counting of immigrants and minorities. Even so, the Bureau itself has estimated that some six million people were missed and perhaps an equal number counted twice. The two errors cancel out as far as total population is concerned, but not, unfortunately, in other respects. The people most likely to have been skipped come from groups that traditionally vote Democratic (this alone insures that the issue will remain alive) and from groups that are often eligible for federal aid. A state can lose federal funding if its eligible populations hve also been undercounted; it may even lose its chance for an additional seat in Congress if the contest is close.

Critics of the census have long argued that the basic head count should be adjusted by applying sampling techniques to identify undercounts and over-counts, but there is some doubt as to whether the sampling techniques are themselves reliable, or whether the public would trust any procedure that is so hard to understand. In the end, the courts decided to rely on the head count alone for reapportionment in 2000 and for the allocation of federal funds, although some states have already announced that they will use sampling techniques of their own when it comes to distributing those funds.

By law the Bureau is required to release a complete count of population, county by county, for the entire nation within a year after the census is taken, so that the work of redistricting can begin. Statistics on minority populations must also be released promptly because minority voting rights are protected by law, and the law cannot be applied unless the courts know the facts. Then, in the years following, the Bureau issues its reports based on the long form. Demographers study the figures and try to decipher the story behind the numbers (who are all these people who are moving to the West? and why are they doing that now?). They pay particular attention to numbers that are unexpected, for these may be indications of a flaw in the model they have been using or the first signs of a shift in social trends.

This book is a collection of articles reprinted from newspapers, magazines, and journals about the population of the United States—what it is and how it may be developing—as represented in the 2000 census. That population is highly diverse, and so are the voices heard here: journalist, scholar, business-woman, activist, private citizen, foreign observer, immigrant. The articles in the first section of the book, "The Census at the End of the Century," establish the context for the 2000 census and examine two of the controversies about the way it was conducted. Articles in Part II, "Who We Are Now," deal with race and ethnic group, age, and gender. In Part III, "Where We Live Now," the subject is the geographical distribution of the populace, and in Part IV, "How We Live Now," it is families and households. Finally, in Part V, "Reapportion-ment and Redistricting," the political implications of the count are explored. Throughout there are maps and tables, some attached to articles, some received directly from the Census Bureau, which also provided a sample of its long form for 2000 and its tally sheet for 1900 (these are reprinted in the Appendix). A Bibliography offers suggestions for additional reading.

In preparing this collection, I was lucky to have a great deal of help. I would like to thank the authors and original publishers of the articles collected here for allowing their works to be reprinted, the Census Bureau for sharing its data, and my colleagues Lynn Messina, Rich Stein, Jennifer Peloso, and San-dra Watson for their assistance, advice, and patience.

Norris Smith
February 2002

I. The Census at the End of the Century

Figure 1

Number of People, 2000

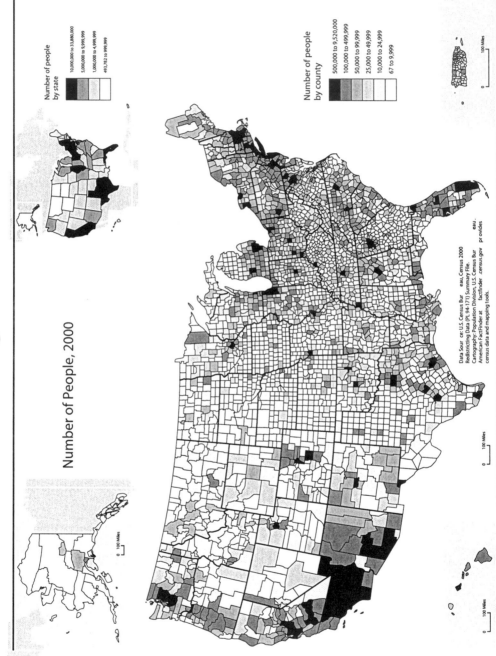

Number of people
by state

10,000,000 to 33,880,000
5,000,000 to 9,999,999
1,000,000 to 4,999,999
493,782 to 999,999

Number of people
by county

500,000 to 9,520,000
100,000 to 499,999
50,000 to 99,999
25,000 to 49,999
10,000 to 24,999
67 to 9,999

0 ___ 100 Miles

0 ___ 100 Miles

0 ___ 100 Miles

Data Sour ce: U.S. Census Bur   eau, Census 2000
Redistricting Data (PL 94-171) Summary File.
Cartography: Population Division, U.S. Census Bur   eau,
American FactFinder at   factfinder .census.gov pr ovides
census data and mapping tools.

Editor's Introduction

The 2000 census, coming as it did at the end of a century, seemed a landmark in America's demographic history, as well as a signpost for the future. Not only has the population of the United States changed over the course of its 224 years, but so too has the census itself, and it will undoubtedly continue to evolve. The census has come a long way since 1790, when "enumerators" fanned out across the country and visited every household, recording the answers to six questions on an oversize sheet of paper printed specially for the purpose. Nowadays, people fill out their own forms, and the questions can total as many as 53. As government has expanded, so has the role of the census, well beyond its original task of determining the makeup of the House of Representatives. Information the Bureau collects is now essential for administering all sorts of programs and allocating billions of dollars in federal funds. Since the stakes are high, the accuracy of the count is of great concern, and the Bureau, which is essentially a scientific agency, must sometimes operate in an atmosphere charged with political passion. As the articles in this section indicate, the way in which the count is conducted may affect the results, and thus can become an issue of controversy.

In "Change and Continuity Since 1900," Louis Hicks places the results of the latest census in the context of a hundred eventful years, tracing the innovations that have transformed American life since 1900 and the constants that have remained. In "The U.S. Just Gets Bigger and Bigger," written for a British audience, Andrew Stephen suggests that America is even more enormous than the Census Bureau can calculate. Stephen is sharply aware of the political and social consequences of an undercount, and he is skeptical of the government's decision to rely on a head count alone, without attempting to adjust for errors. This controversy is reported in dispassionate detail in Eric Schmitt's "Bid for Altered Census Figures Is Rejected"; it is a dispute likely to be reignited in 2010. Finally, in "Utah Defends Missionaries," Alyssa Rayman-Read provides a concise account of the issues between Utah and North Carolina in their battle over one seat in Congress, a quarrel that went all the way to the Supreme Court and, like the dispute over the head count, may influence the shape of censuses to come.

Change and Continuity Since 1900[1]

By Louis Hicks
World & I, May 2001

From 1900 to 2000, the United States underwent dramatic changes but also demonstrated strong continuities. The material standard of living rose at least eightfold, but the prevalence of religious observance and belief changed very little. While the federal government increased its programs enormously, the suicide rate was the same at the beginning and end of the century. These and other details are revealed in a new study, *The First Measured Century*.

The population rose from 76 million, counted in the 1900 census, to 281 million, reported in 2000. Part of this increase came from high birthrates at the beginning of the century and during the baby boom (1946–1964). Another big reason for the population increase was a sharp increase in life expectancy: from about 50 years in 1900 to around 76 years in 2000. The population was also augmented by two great waves of immigration: The first wave, lasting until 1924, was drawn mainly from southern and eastern Europe; the second wave, beginning in 1965, came mainly from Latin America and Asia.

Americans drifted westward throughout the century so that the population shares of the Midwest and Northeast declined, while that of the West rose. Americans also changed their residential patterns, moving from farms to cities in the early decades of the century, then from cities to suburbs after World War II. Contrary to widespread belief, Americans do not move more often than they used to: in 1948, one in five moved, but in 1999, only one in six moved.

Changes in work

In 1900, a plurality (42 percent) of American men worked in primary occupations such as farming and fishing; by 1998, only 4 percent did. The big growth was in tertiary-sector occupations such as management and service (from 21 percent to 58 percent). Interestingly, the proportion working in secondary occupations (such as factory work) was exactly the same in 1998 as it had been in 1900 (38

---

1. Article by Louis Hicks from *World & I* May 2001. Copyright © *World & I*. Reprinted with permission.

percent). Work became much safer—the annual death toll on railroads and in coal mines, for example, dropped from about 5,000 early in the century to about 100 today.

Contrary to another widespread impression, the amount of housework done by American women plummeted. In 1924, Robert and Helen Lynd found that 87 percent of housewives in Middletown (Muncie, Indiana) averaged four or more hours of housework per day. They baked bread, made the family's clothes, canned their own food, and did the laundry by hand. When the First Measured Century project repeated the Lynds' study in 1999, we found that only 14 percent of Middletown housewives said they did four or more daily hours of housework. Store-bought foods, electrical appliances, and wash-and-wear fabrics, among other improvements, had done away with an entire tradition of drudgery.

With fewer children and much less housework, American women poured into the labor force.

With fewer children and much less housework, American women poured into the labor force. In 1900, 6 percent of married women were in the labor force; by 1998, it was 61 percent. Initially, women were restricted to particular occupations and to the lower ranks of other jobs. These barriers gradually eroded so that by 2000, about half of all managers, administrators, government officials, psychologists, and accountants were women.

The shift from digging and hammering to filling out forms and negotiating agreements required a massive upgrading of workers' skills. This was accomplished by a huge increase in education. In 1910, 13 percent of adults had at least a high school education. By 1998, 83 percent of adults had at least that much education.

Surprisingly, most (60 percent) of the high-school graduates in 1900 were women. (Men dropped out to go to work.) Education expanded in every way possible: children started school at earlier ages and stayed much longer; a much greater proportion finished college; graduate school became the normal path to professional jobs such as lawyer and doctor; and Harvard tuition rose sevenfold (after adjusting for inflation).

Marriage, sex, and fertility

Americans are among the world's most marrying peoples. While this remained true throughout the twentieth century, the circumstances changed. The average age at first marriage in 1900 was 22 for women and 26 for men. Then it declined until around 1960, when it started climbing, reaching 25 for women and 27 for men in 1996.

The divorce rate rose from about 4 per thousand married women per year to around 20 per thousand per year. Incidentally, this does not imply that half of all today's marriages will end in divorce. If present trends continue, about one-third to 40 percent of marriages may end in divorce.

Sexuality changed along with marriage patterns. Premarital sex was rare in 1900 (only 6 percent of 19-year-old women) but common in 1991 (74 percent). Cohabitation was almost unheard-of before 1960 but is now the common pattern before marriage.

But polls suggest that extramarital sex is less common today than earlier in the century. Attitudes reflect this change in behavior. In 1972, 27 percent of adults agreed that sex before marriage was "not wrong at all." In 1996, 44 percent agreed. Premarital sex received some approval but extramarital sex was universally condemned: in 1972, 4 percent thought it was "not wrong at all" and in 1996, 2 percent thought so.

The total fertility rate (TFR) is the average number of children a woman has in her lifetime. The TFR rode a roller coaster during the century. In 1905, women had an average of 3.8 children. In the Great Depression, this figure fell to just above two. During the baby boom, the average number of children rose back up to 3.8. After 1970, the TFR fell below the level required to maintain the size of the U.S. population and has stayed below that level for 30 years.

These changes in marriage, sex, and fertility may be thought to reflect disconnections. Sex was disconnected from marriage in the sense that premarital sex was no longer widely condemned and "living together" before marriage became common. Sex was disconnected from fertility by technological advances in birth control. Marriage was disconnected from fertility because an increasing number of women bore and raised children outside of marriage.

In 1924, virtually all high-school students in Middletown lived with both natural parents. In 1977, about three-quarters of them lived with both parents. In 1999, only one-half lived with both parents. But parents were spending more time with their children. In 1924, 60 percent of Middletown fathers averaged at least an hour a day with their children; by 1977, this figure had reached 81 percent; in 1999, it was 83 percent.

Higher standard of living

Perhaps the biggest change in Americans' daily lives was in their household standard of living—U.S. housing was dramatically upgraded during the century. It is hard for us to conceive of housing conditions in 1900: no central heating, no running water, no electricity.

Imagine living in a two-car garage with five other people and utilities limited to a wood stove, gas lights, a well with a hand pump, and an outhouse. Now think of the rush of inventions that transformed the home: electricity, central heating, indoor plumbing, washing machine and dryer, a refrigerator, air-conditioning, radio, television, a telephone, and a personal computer. And the little garage grew into a two-story house with a separate room for each person.

It is hard for us to conceive of housing conditions in 1900: no central heating, no running water, no electricity.

Then the garage became the home for the family car and later for the family cars. In 1900, there were 8,000 automobiles. By 1930, most families had one; by the end of the century, many families had two or more.

The private automobile is now the primary means of transportation for most of the U.S. population. Annual travel by all U.S. motor vehicles rose 25,600-fold over the century. This led to traffic jams and smog but also to an unprecedented freedom of mobility. The annual number of visitors to Yellowstone National Park rose from 13,727 in 1904 to 3.1 million in 1998.

Religion showed strong continuities but also important changes. Weekly attendance at religious services was remarkably stable: 43 percent went in 1939, compared to 40 percent in 1998. The proportion of the population that believes in God has fluctuated between 95 and 99 percent. Protestants saw a shift from mainstream denominations such as Methodist to more evangelical denominations such as Southern Baptist and a decline in the overall Protestant share of the population.

The Roman Catholic proportion of the population rose from 13 to 23 percent. Other religions also grew: Eastern Orthodoxy, the Latter-Day Saints, and Islam registered large gains. The Jewish proportion remained roughly stable at around 2 percent. Ecumenical attitudes rose: in 1924, 91 percent of Middletown high-school students thought that Christianity was "the one true religion and all peoples should be converted to it"; in 1999, only 42 percent were so inclined.

The health and safety of Americans improved radically during the twentieth century. Improvements in nutrition, sanitation, and heating, coupled with new vaccines and therapies eliminated a score of diseases that afflicted millions of Americans a century ago. But all was not perfect. People who escaped polio and whooping cough lived long enough to contract heart disease and cancer—progress against these conditions has been slower. And sexually transmitted diseases have spread because promiscuity outpaced medical advances.

Cigarette consumption—our most significant voluntary health risk—increased from 54 cigarettes per capita in 1900 to a peak near 4,000 in 1964, when the first Surgeon General's Report on Smoking and Health was issued; thereafter, smoking declined about 50 per-

---

The health and safety of Americans improved radically during the twentieth century.

---

cent by 1999. Illegal drug use, especially of marijuana, rose in the 1960s, then declined, then rose again in the 1990s. Safety improvements throughout society have led to an 80 percent decline in the accidental death rate.

Growth in income and government

The real incomes (adjusted for inflation) of American workers increased dramatically during the century. As their incomes rose, American families spent a smaller share of their budget on food (43 percent in 1900 to 15 percent in 1997) and a larger share on transportation (2 percent in 1900 to 12 percent in 1997). They also gave away more money: philanthropic donations (not including bequests) increased twelve-fold in real dollars from 1930 to 1990.

The increase in standard of living was greater for the poor than for the rich: the incomes of the lowest 40 percent of families tripled from 1929 to 1998, while the incomes of the top 5 percent almost doubled. Likewise, the proportion of the population living below the official poverty line fell from 22 percent in 1959 to 12 percent in 1999.

Votes in presidential elections were almost evenly divided over the century between Democratic and Republican candidates. Contrary to popular impression, voter turnout shows little sign of decline: the voter participation rate in 2000 was about the same as in 1920. Democrats held more seats in Congress during the century, with their biggest majorities during the Depression and the Cold War. The number of women in Congress increased from zero in 1900 to 65 in 1999.

> *Government grew faster than other parts of American society.*

Government grew faster than other parts of American society. From 1900 to 1999, federal government expenditures rose from 3 to 19 percent of the gross domestic product. State and local governments saw a similar increase. But the federal government employed a lower proportion of the labor force in 1997 than it did at any time since before World War II.

Why did federal expenditures grow while the number of federal government employees has shrunk? The answer is an enormous growth in entitlements, payments by the government to (or on behalf of) individuals.

In 1900, these consisted of a few disbursements to veterans or their widows. In 1996, these payments reached most of the population. Some of the biggest programs were Social Security, Medicare, Medicaid, and TANF (Temporary Assistance for Needy Families), but the list was practically endless: school lunches, disaster relief, unemployment insurance, and so forth.

While the proportion of federal employees did not increase, the number of workers in the federal judiciary quadrupled from 1960 to 1998, as did the number of cases handled in federal courts every year. Federal judges became involved in dozens of areas of social life: child care, product safety, environmental salvage, museum management, and worker-employer disputes, to name only a few.

Military beefs up; crime rate rises

In 1900, the United States had a small army and navy with only 126,000 men on active duty. A huge mobilization for World War I was followed by an almost total demobilization. A much larger mobilization for World War II (16 million Americans) was followed by the maintenance of a large permanent armed force.

In 1900, the armed forces were composed almost entirely of white men, but by century's end, blacks made up 30 percent of enlistees of the U.S. Army and women constituted 14 percent of the overall armed forces. American casualties in the two world wars were much lighter than those of other countries; this contributed to America's postwar economic success relative to Europe and Japan.

Crime rates rose and fell throughout the century, with peaks in the 1920s and '30s and in the 1970s and '80s. The incarceration rate fluctuated until 1980, when it began an unprecedented rise from

139 per 100,000 people in 1980 to 462 per 100,000 in 1999—a rate never before reached in a developed country. The increase in the number of prisoners reflected mandatory minimum sentences, reduced parole, and energetic prosecution of the "war on drugs."

The economy grew and stabilized during the century. From 1900 to 1999, the per-capita output of the economy grew from $4,256 to $34,565 (adjusted for inflation). Annual swings in the business cycle of 10 percent were common before World War II; not a single one of that size occurred after the war.

In this more stable environment, American business grew by leaps and bounds. Business revenue increased ninefold from 1939 to 1996, while the population only doubled. This increase was reflected in stock trading volume (up 1,300-fold since 1939), the value of stocks (Dow Jones Industrial Average up 77-fold since 1939), and the proportion of households owning stocks (from 4 percent in 1952 to 52 percent in 1998).

Most of the increase in economic output was due to technological innovations. New patents rose from 25,000 per year in 1901 to 168,000 per year in 1999. As the U.S. economy expanded, its connections to the rest of the world became more important. Adjusting for population growth, imports and exports of goods increased about tenfold from 1900 to 1999; imports and exports of services increased about fourfold from 1960 to 1999. U.S. investments abroad and foreign investments in the United States rose dramatically. In 1999, foreign investments in the United States were worth $31,688 per American, while U.S. investments abroad amounted to $26,286 per American.

Americans communicated with one another more as the century went on. The number of new book titles published increased from 6,000 per year in 1900 to 65,000 in 1997. The average American got about 150 pieces of mail a year in 1900 and about 1,100 pieces in 1998; telephone calls increased even more, from 38 per person to 2,325 per person per year. Newspaper circulation grew from 1900 to about midcentury, when a long, slow decline began as afternoon papers lost out to television.

From periphery to center

In 1900, the United States was one of about a dozen world powers and by no means the most important. It wasn't the richest, the biggest, or the most powerful, and it was located on the periphery of the world. Today, it is a gross understatement to say that the situation has changed.

The United States is the greatest power the world has yet seen. U.S. armed forces are so powerful that direct military confrontation with the United States is impossible for any other country. The U.S.

economy is the dynamic center of an emerging world economy. The U.S. dollar functions as the reserve currency for the entire world. American living standards continue to rise at least as fast as anywhere else on earth. New technological advances continue to pour forth from the United States: cell phones, the Internet, mapping the human genome, and many more. American culture is so wildly popular that other countries pass laws against it. English has become the lingua franca of the whole planet.

The principles of America's founding political documents are widely imitated. The United States continues to be the world destination for ambitious, capable immigrants in every field. America has become the world's first hyperpower, combining financial, economic, political, military, and cultural priority. Only time will tell what will come of this overwhelming dominance.

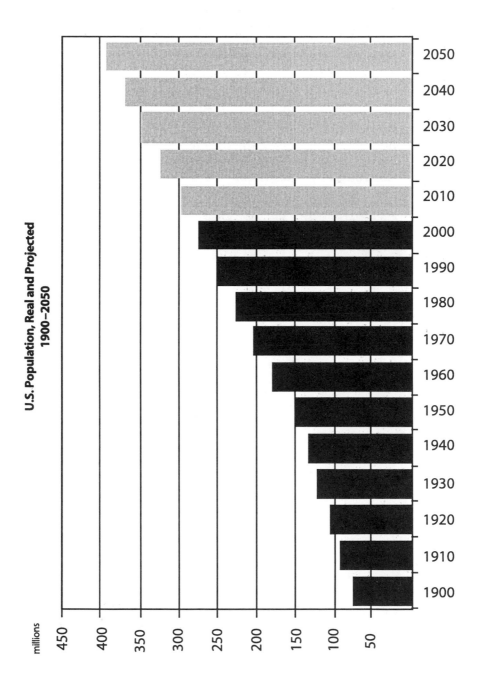

Figure 2

U.S. Population, Real and Projected
1900–2050

The U.S. Just Gets Bigger and Bigger[2]

BY ANDREW STEPHEN
NEW STATESMAN, FEBRUARY 5, 2001

Just under a year ago, I was plagued by endless letters and even personal callers deluging the house where I then lived. Britons who idealize the U.S. often fail to realize that it can be a country of staggering bureaucratic incompetence—the 2000 presidential election showed the world just a glimpse of that—and the 2000 U.S. census, even though it was bolstered by a $168 million advertising campaign, was fairly typical. Neither computers nor humans could understand my fairly routine situation: I was then living in one house but about to move into another, which was empty. The system couldn't cope with the notion of a temporarily empty house—and, despite explanations both in writing and face to face with officials, I kept receiving stern orders to provide details of everybody living in the empty house.

It seemed merely exasperating at the time but, now the preliminary results of last year's census have come out, the consequences of such bureaucratic bungling have come home to me. The U.S. population has jumped 13.2 percent since 1990 to 281,421,906 (more than 55 times the population when the first census was taken in 1790). This is five million more than statistical experts predicted three months ago. More to the point, it is likely that around ten million people were not counted at all, while about half that number were counted twice—as I would have been, had I not resisted. Those not counted, inevitably, tended to be the poor, country dwellers, minorities and children; those counted twice tended to have two homes (as I did, albeit temporarily).

In other words, both state and federal governments are operating on brand-new data that, none the less, underestimates the prevalence of those most needing help. The 1990 census missed 250,000 people in Florida, which deprived the state of $2 billion in federal funds. Now Governor Jeb Bush must await word from Big Brother George to see whether the federal government will make up what is likely to prove a considerably larger shortfall in 2000. He will, we can safely assume, be waiting forever. Everything militates against action now: in 1999, the right-wing Supreme Court deemed it illegal for states to use statistical projections rather than the literal data of the censuses. Florida is the seventh most rapidly expanding state in the country—gaining 834 new people every day—but, with its large elderly and poor immigrant population, is also one where social services will be under more and more stress.

Indeed, the first data from the 2000 census—more demographic data will come out next month—turns out, like so many things American, to have major political repercussions. It showed that, with the steady decline of manufacturing industry, there is a slowing in the rate of population growth in the north-east and midwest—meaning that states such as Connecticut, New York, Pennsylvania, Ohio, Indiana, Michigan, Illinois and Wisconsin will all lose seats by the time the midterm Congressional elections are held in 2002. It is mandated by a 1911 law (not, as many think, by the Constitution) that there be 435 House members, and their constituencies have to be sized according to the whereabouts of the population.

This is a country changing demographically and racially at an unprecedented speed.

In this case, the trend over the past two decades has been towards the south and west, with states such as Nevada (whose population has jumped 66.3 percent since 1990), Arizona (40 percent), Colorado (30.6 percent) and Texas (22.8 percent) emerging as big winners. I offer no prizes for the obvious conclusion: the states losing out are either Democratic or marginal; those rapidly expanding tend to be Republican. The Republicans believe that, because of population shifts, they are likely to win between ten and 14 new seats in the 2002 elections. Put another way, states won by Bush last year will probably gain an extra seven electoral college votes; states won by Gore will lose seven.

The explosion in the population here (one in ten people was born outside the U.S.) has yet further political ramifications. Because Congress insists on sticking to the 1911 figure of 435 Representatives (when the population of the U.S. was a third of what it is today), politicians in Washington are becoming increasingly remote from day-to-day life in the areas they represent. The first Congress had roughly one Congressman for every 60,000 Americans; men and women taking office in the 108th Congress in 2003 will each represent around 650,000. They are thus unable to operate effective, British-style political surgeries* (MPs in England and Wales represent, on average, 100,000 people each) and become known to constituents largely via the media, rather than through personal contact.

---

* Home offices.

What is most striking about the 2000 census, however, is that the population in almost all of the 50 states is still rapidly increasing; only in my neck of the woods, in D.C., was the population recorded as decreasing, by 5.7 percent. America, people tend to forget, is still fast-growing: in 1900, there were just 528,542 people in Florida; today, the state's population is nearly 16 million, only three million or so short of the entire continent of Australia. At nearly 34 million, California's population is more than double that of Florida.

The demographic and racial information released next month will be the most fascinating of all, however. It is likely to reflect an America that few Britons realize is fast emerging, confirming that, from Hawaii to California to Houston to New York, no single race now has an outright majority. In little more than 50 years, whites will be outnumbered by other races. This is a country changing demographically and racially at an unprecedented speed—which is why the taking of accurate censuses will become increasingly crucial, politically and socially. Let us hope they remember that in 2010.

Bid for Altered Census Figures Is Rejected[3]

By Eric Schmitt
New York Times, October 18, 2001

The Census Bureau said today that it would not adjust the 2000 population tally for use in allocating billions of dollars in annual federal aid across the country.

The decision means that the federal government will use the raw head count available now to allocate federal aid for Medicaid, foster care and other social service programs. About $185 billion a year was distributed based on population counts from the 1990 census.

The Census Bureau and a number of Democrats and liberal groups have clashed for months over whether to adjust the 2000 census figures to make up for millions of uncounted people, mainly racial minorities and renters.

At a news conference today, William G. Barron Jr., the acting director of the Census Bureau, said the agency rejected using adjusted data for distributing federal money because the data had too many errors to be reliable.

In March, the bureau said it missed at least 6.4 million people last year and counted at least 3.1 million twice. Mr. Barron said today that enumerators may have double-counted an additional 3 million.

As was the case in 1990, the adjusted numbers for the 2000 census were produced by a survey, in this case one involving 314,000 households, conducted by the bureau after the traditional decennial count was completed. The final count was 281.4 million.

In both 1990 and last year, the survey showed the extent to which the census missed millions of people or double-counted others, mainly whites and homeowners. Earlier this year, the Bush administration decided to use the raw head count for the purposes of redrawing Congressional districts.

Many big-city mayors reacted angrily to that decision.

"It is unfair and unwise," said Mayor Marc H. Morial of New Orleans, the president of the United States Conference of Mayors. "Cities now stand to lose hundreds of millions of dollars in federal as well as state aid over the next decade."

A spokesman for Mayor Rudolph W. Giuliani of New York sounded a more resigned note. "We were expecting the administration to use a straight head count, so it was not a surprise to us," said Sid Dinsay, a spokesman for Mr. Giuliani.

Today's decision does not end the dispute. Critics of the Census Bureau are demanding that it immediately release the adjusted data for areas as small as city blocks for all 50 states.

On Thursday, a lawsuit begins in Federal District Court in Portland, Ore., in which two Oregon state senators are seeking to compel the government to release the detailed data.

"Cities and planning offices would love to look at the numbers to assess them and better understand them, so they can design better social service programs and the delivery of them," said Veronique Pluviose-Fenton, principal legislative counsel for the National League of Cities in Washington.

But in a telephone interview today, John H. Thompson, director of the 2000 census, rejected the cities' pleas. "We have no immediate plans to release block-level data," Mr. Thompson said. "It's just too flawed."

Kenneth Prewitt, the census director in the Clinton administration, defended the bureau's decision today, saying that the "data is driving the decision." But Mr. Prewitt urged census officials to release the block-level data for scientific review.

Census officials insisted again today that despite the total number of errors in the 2000 census—12.5 million people missed or counted twice, just below the 12.8 million errors in 1990—the latest count was the most accurate in American history.

The bureau had said there was a net national undercount of 1.2 percent of the country's 281.4 million people in 2000, or about 3.3 million. The 1990 undercount was 1.6 percent, or about 4 million.

Mr. Barron said today, however, that estimates showed the net undercount in 2000 was reduced to less than 1 percent. He said poverty and unemployment measurements that had long used adjusted data could rely on the more accurate head count.

Working with the sampling data, census officials said the head count had missed 0.6 percent of the overall population, compared with 1.61 percent in 1990; 0.8 percent of blacks compared with 4.57 percent; and 1.25 percent of Hispanics, compared with nearly 5 percent.

But Mr. Barron said the bureau had also probably double-counted hundreds of thousands of non-Hispanic whites, a finding that drew criticisms from minority rights groups.

"They're adding whites who don't exist and leaving out minorities who are consistently passed over," said Karen K. Narasaki, executive director of National Asian Pacific American Legal Consortium, an advocacy group. "Our concern is to use adjusted numbers for federal allocations to poor people."

Utah Defends Missionaries[4]

By Alyssa Rayman-Read
American Prospect, February 26, 2001

Conservative leaders in Utah do not want to follow the rules of Florida math—that is, the precept that the first count is the best one, no matter how incomplete. The state of Utah, led by its Republican governor and five congressmen, has filed suit in federal court demanding a recount of census 2000 numbers. The problem: Utah came up just short of having enough people to win a new congressional seat. By an Al Gore-style margin of 856 people, Utah lost out to North Carolina.

Utah officials want the Census Bureau's count to include the state's 14,000 Mormon missionaries living abroad. Or if missionaries aren't counted, they argue, military and civil service personnel stationed overseas should not be tallied. (North Carolina's 18,360 troops and diplomats stationed abroad trounced the Beehive State's 3,545.)

Counting people, it turns out, is as politically charged as counting votes. Arguing that the Constitution requires an "actual enumeration," conservatives have long battled census officials' attempts to use "sampling methods" in achieving a national head count. The stakes are high because census figures are used not just to apportion the 435 seats in the U.S. House of Representatives but to allocate federal funds to states and municipalities. Because the decennial census tends to undercount populations in Democratic areas, some on the right fear that statistical sampling will drive those numbers up.

And the Census Bureau has been inconsistent about counting U.S. citizens living overseas. Only the 1970, 1990, and 2000 surveys "officially" included military and federal employees stationed abroad and their dependents. Utah officials maintain that making distinctions between categories of Americans who live outside the country's borders is unfair. "Missionaries are unique in some respects," Utah Governor Mike Leavitt told *The Salt Lake Tribune*, but in their need for political representation, "they are identical to those serving in the military or civil service overseas."

Of course, it's easier to count federal employees. What kind of sampling techniques might be necessary to count missionaries and others temporarily out of the country? How accurate will those counts be? The Census Bureau maintains that it lacks the resources to count all private citizens abroad. As well, Census Director Kenneth Prewitt points out that "if you count Utah's missionaries, you must count the missionaries belonging to every other state." Then there are college students and business people stationed abroad. And how do you tell a permanent emigrant from a U.S. resident on hiatus?

Finally, there is the high conservative principle against altering rules at the end of the count. "If the courts find that Utah's missionaries should be included in the 2000 census tally, every other state would sue us," contends Prewitt. "This is a fair criticism of the census, one which could be considered for the 2010 survey, but you can't change the rules after the game."

If the case ever reaches the Supreme Court, oddsmakers might want to check whether Justice Antonin Scalia has closer ties to Utah than he does to North Carolina.

Editor's note: On November 27, 2001, the Supreme Court upheld, without comment, a lower court's decision that Utah had no constitutional case.

II. Who We Are Now

Figure 3

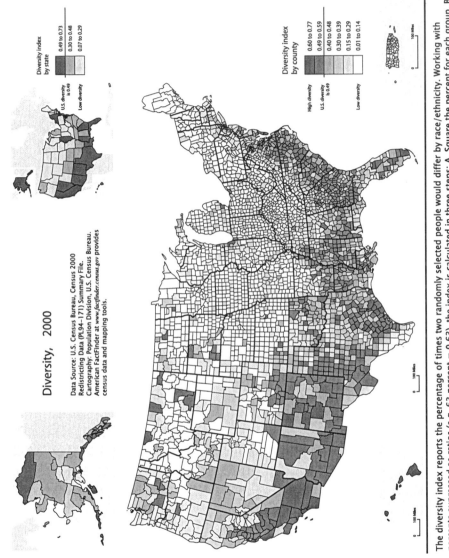

Diversity, 2000

Data Source: U.S. Census Bureau, Census 2000 Redistricting Data (PL94–171) Summary File.
Cartography: Population Division, U.S. Census Bureau. American FactFinder at *www.factfinder.census.gov* provides census data and mapping tools.

Diversity index by state

U.S. diversity to 0.49	0.49 to 0.73
	0.30 to 0.48
Low diversity	0.07 to 0.29

Diversity index by county

High diversity	0.60 to 0.77
U.S. diversity to 0.49	0.49 to 0.59
	0.40 to 0.48
	0.30 to 0.39
	0.15 to 0.29
Low diversity	0.01 to 0.14

The diversity index reports the percentage of times two randomly selected people would differ by race/ethnicity. Working with percents expressed as ratios (e.g. 63 percent = 0.63), the index is calculated in three steps: A. Square the percent for each group. B. Sum the squares, and C. Subtract the sum from 1.00. Eight groups were used for the index: 1. White, not Hispanic; 2. Black or African American; 3. American Indian and Alaska Native (AIAN); 4. Asian; 5. Native Hawaiian and Other Pacific Islander (NHOP); 6. Two or more races, not Hispanic; 7. Some other race, not Hispanic; and 8. Hispanic or Latino. People indicating Hispanic origin who also indicated Black, AIAN, Asian, or NHOPI were counted only in their race group (0.5 percent of the population). They were not included in the Hispanic group.

Editor's Introduction

The great surprise of the census was the explosion in the number of Hispanics in the United States—58 percent more than were recorded in 1990. The Hispanic population has grown so rapidly that it is now on a par with the African American population in the United States, a development that left demographers scrambling to redo their calculations and provoked extensive discussion over the possibility of a truly multiracial society. The census also showed an advance in the median age of Americans, which surprised no one, since the baby boomers—the largest generation—are now ten years older than they were in 1990, and confirmed the existence of a substantial, though less sharply defined, "echo boom." The ratio of men to women also changed, moving the genders a little closer to demographic equality. The articles in this section center on ethnicity, race, age, and gender, characteristics of basic identity, as delineated by the 2000 census.

In "The Many Faces of America," Michael Barone describes the increasingly visible influence of Hispanics on the American scene, the factors that draw immigrants to the U.S. from Latin America, and the prospects for eventual assimilation. U.S.-born Hispanics particularly, Barone reports, seem poised to enter an American mainstream that is itself being changed by their presence. That not all Hispanics are finding it easy or even possible to move from the *barrio* toward a full participation in American life is evident from Kristin Anderson Moore's "Time to Take a Closer Look at Hispanic Children and Families," published in *Policy and Practice*, a social services journal, which outlines some of daunting problems afflicting a large section of the Hispanic population. In "Hispanic Catholics: 'El futuro' Is Here," Timothy Matovina describes a different assimilation problem, as the American Catholic Church, built and largely staffed by people of European ancestry, struggles to accommodate a burgeoning Latino congregation and its distinctive culture.

The emergence of a new ethnic minority—Hispanics—comparable in population to the older African American minority (whose long exclusion from equality has been a focus for social action since the sixties) has led to serious reappraisal of the role of minorities in American life. As Roberto Suro observed, in a 1998 article for the *Washington Post*,

> Now the question is whether Latino and Asian newcomers and their offspring will end up on the "white" side of the color line, thus disastrously hardening the exclusion of blacks, or on the "black" side, meaning that they could be excluded too. I hold hope for another possibility: This wave of immigration might spark a process of social change that blurs, perhaps

even erases, the sharp division between black and white that has scarred the nation's soul since its founding. ("The Next Wave: How Immigration Blurs the Race Discussion," *Washington Post*, July 19, 1998)

This is a hope cautiously endorsed by Nathan Glazer, who, in "American Diversity and the 2000 Census," sees a real possibility that the entire system of racial and ethnic tabulation developed in this country may ultimately collapse of its own weight. At present, however, he believes that the old patterns are still with us, albeit in weakened form. He traces the history of America's obsession with race as evidenced on census forms from earliest times, the emergence (or construction) of the four "official" minorities that the government recognizes today, and the complications introduced by the 2000 census, the first to allow people to list themselves as members of more than one race. One person who did that, Lise Funderburg, was inspired by the census questions to write "I Am What I say I Am," an essay that shows what multiracial ancestry may mean to an individual. From quite a different perspective, some of the practical problems posed by the new methods of counting are discussed by Jo Ann S. Barefoot in "Melting Pot or Salad Bowl?" an article addressed to the banking industry, which is eager to attract minority customers but anxious to avoid the sort of legal actions brought against it in the past, over discrimination in lending and hiring. Then, looking ahead to a future when no group will constitute a majority, Laurent Belsie investigates a new academic specialty, in "Scholars Unearth New Field: White Studies," and interviews some of its advocates.

Ethnicity and race are not the only factors that interest demographers. The 2000 census confirmed that the median age of the American population is gradually advancing and would be advancing even faster were it not for a steady influx of immigrants. At the same time, Americans are living longer, thanks to medical advances and healthier lifestyles. Seniors account for 12 percent of the American population overall, and their numbers are expected to swell over the next twenty years. In "The New Seniors," Jay Rey researches the Buffalo/Niagara metropolitan area in upstate New York, where the senior population has already reached percentages that other cities will not see for another decade. To keep this spirited population as independent as possible, Buffalo/Niagara needs more affordable housing, transportation, meals on wheels, and a host of other services. At the other end of the age curve, cities like Houston are experiencing a surge in high school students (the "echo boom") as well as an unforeseen influx of grade-schoolers, the children of young couples who have moved to the Sunbelt from other parts of the country or from Mexico. This is the topic of Genaro C. Armas's "Wave of School-Age Children to Flood Nation's Classrooms." Finally, Laurent Belsie analyzes America's male/female ratio in "Men Make a Numerical Comeback" and compares it with the gender profiles of other nations.

The Many Faces of America[1]

By Michael Barone
U.S. News & World Report, March 19, 2001

Westfield Middle School, located among the well-tended and nearly all-white suburbs north of Indianapolis, enrolled its first student studying English as a second language in 1998. Now the school employs a full-time teaching assistant to aid students who arrive speaking only Spanish. "So many of our Hispanic students are new arrivals," says Ed Mendoza, the school's principal. "We're just trying to help them get connected." A few miles south, the annual Fiesta Indianapolis had 35,000 people turn up last September, nearly double the number of three years before. And, unlike in past years, Fiesta had no trouble attracting corporate sponsors. "We don't have to go looking for them anymore," says organizer Carmen DeRusha. "They're coming to us. Soft-drink companies, banks, major grocery stores—they all want to be involved."

Similar signs of the changing face of America can be found all over the place. Hispanics are streaming into the Hoosier state—and most of the other 49 states as well; the number of Hispanics doubled in states like Virginia and Wisconsin. In Hamilton County, where Westfield sits, the Hispanic population has increased 143 percent in 10 years. Behind the dry columns of numbers in last week's Census Bureau population report lies a story of a profound and dramatic change in American life. Census takers last year counted 35.3 million Hispanics—1 out of 8 people in the United States—an astonishing 58 percent increase over the 22.4 million Hispanics counted 10 years earlier. The number of Hispanics here today is greater than the entire population of Canada. It's also, for the first time, more than the 34.7 million people who identify themselves as black. An additional 1.7 million said they were partly black and partly another race.

Hispanics have now become—or are on the verge of becoming—the nation's largest minority group. And with that, our ideas of what a minority group is are bound to change. "Hispanic" is a government-invented term for people of Latin American or Spanish descent or Spanish-language background. There are no clear criteria to determine who is Hispanic; census takers simply accept a person's self-description.

---

1. Article by Michael Barone from *U.S. News & World Report* March 19, 2001. Copyright © U.S. News & World Report, L.P. Reprinted with permission.

The emerging portrait of America's self-image in 2001 is one that could closely resemble that of a century ago, when immigrants from many lands arrived at Ellis Island. Once again, perhaps, we will see ourselves as a nation of people of many different origins. Indeed, the Census Bureau now allows for 63 different biracial classifications.

Why have so many Hispanics come to the United States? In a word: work.

Kids at home. The huge increase in the Hispanic population is mostly the result of large immigration flows from Mexico and other parts of Latin America. Many come only to work and expect to return home; only 7 percent of those who arrived in the 1990s have become U.S. citizens. Still, partly because children born here are automatically citizens, about 70 percent of Hispanics have American citizenship. And Hispanics have plenty of children; 31 percent of Hispanic households have five or more people, compared with 12 percent among non-Hispanic whites. Over 70 percent of Hispanics are under 40, which means that even if immigration were suddenly to stop, the Hispanic percentage of the nation's population would continue to rise.

Why have so many Hispanics come to the United States? In a word: work. And a powerful work ethic. Workforce participation among Hispanic males is 80 percent, the highest of any measured group. "You go to New York," says Antonio Martinez, an immigrant from Puebla, Mexico, "to work, eat, and sleep." Even those in poverty receive welfare far less often than poor blacks or whites. Though many work in low-wage jobs, the Association of Hispanic Advertising Agencies says Hispanic household incomes have been growing 7.5 percent per year over the past five years.

And while poverty rates among Hispanics remain high, the numbers also mask the progress of long-established immigrants and U.S.-born Latinos. Ten years ago, most of America's Hispanics were concentrated in a few big metropolitan areas in California, Texas, Florida, New York, New Jersey, and Illinois. But in the past decade immigrants from Latin America and U.S.-born Hispanics have been appearing in large numbers in places they have never been seen before, particularly in the nation's iconic suburbs. Thousands have moved to small factory towns on the Great Plains to work in meatpacking plants. But they have also moved to places like the red clay hills of north Georgia. The Hispanic population of booming Gwinnett County, outside Atlanta, increased from 8,000 in 1990 to over 26,000 in 1999. On the main drag, Buford Highway, you can find the El Expreso Bus Co., Los Ranchos Restaurant, or Carniceria Hispana. While low-wage jobs are the early magnet for many, there is also evidence of decidedly upward mobility. Homero Luna left Mexico for Dalton, Ga., and a job in the poultry factory's killing line. Now, at 27, he is the owner of the weekly tabloid *El Tiempo*, with a circulation of 28,000 in north Georgia. And there are many others. "For every 10 Latinos I see driving around in trucks, I know 3 of them own their own little companies," says Sam Zamarripa, head of HispanB2B in Atlanta. "They are completely entrepreneurial."

And religious. Hispanics have swelled the numbers of American Catholics; for the past decade, Los Angeles's Cardinal Roger Mahony has required that all priests in the archdiocese be fluent in Spanish as well as English. Immigrants from Latin America tend to have little education; nearly half of adult Hispanics have not graduated from high school. But the reasons are complex, and finding solutions to that problem will be one of the fundamental challenges of the nation's education system.

Language remains a barrier, but the desire to learn English is clearly there. Spanish-language TV has developed a large audience in the United States, with programming dominated by *telenovelas* produced in Mexico and other Latin countries. But the audience for Spanish broadcasting is made up almost entirely of adults. Children and teenagers prefer the English-language programs that others their age watch.

And in many respects, Hispanics are no more homogeneous in their tastes than blacks and whites. Programmers have found that Mexican entertainment does not appeal to Cubans in Miami or

---

Strength in numbers

Hispanics surpassed blacks as a share of the total U.S. population, according to the 2000 census.

Share of total U.S. population

	1990	2000
Hispanics	9%	12.5%
Blacks	12.1%	12.3%

National origin of Hispanics in the U.S.

Central/South America	14.5%
Puerto Rico	9%
Cuba	4%
Other	6.4%
Mexico	66.1%

Note: Hispanics may be of any race.
Source: U.S. Census Bureau

Puerto Ricans in the New York area. Tejano music is dynamite in Texas but not in California, whose technobanda music does not sell elsewhere. Univision news anchor Jorge Ramos, a Mexican citizen, has worked to develop a Spanish accent that does not sound jarring to Cubans, Puerto Ricans, and Central and South Americans. Diversity among Hispanics is also evident in their politics. Hispanics have developed political preferences based on where they came from and where they have settled, though Democrats still captured a clear majority of the Hispanic vote in 2000 despite George W. Bush's considerable efforts at outreach.

What we are seeing is not so much the emergence of one new minority group but of a population made up, as America always has been, of people with a variety of backgrounds and origins.

Time to Take a Closer Look at Hispanic Children and Families[2]

By Kristin Anderson Moore
Policy and Practice, June 2001

The census results for the nation's Hispanic population seem to have taken many people by surprise. It's not that they did not expect the 2000 census to show growth in this population. They just did not expect that growth to be so large and to have occurred so swiftly—so fast that the numbers of Hispanics and African Americans in the nation are now just about equal.

What do we know about this booming population? For many Americans, the answer is, "Surprisingly little." They are aware that there are more Spanish-speaking people in their communities. But they do not know very much about what is going on in the lives of the Hispanic families they see and hear about.

At Child Trends, we track statistics on children and families. In the course of this work, we have noticed both warning flags and encouraging signs behind the explosive growth in the Hispanic population. What are some of the warning flags? Consider these measures of child and family well-being:

- Education: Hispanics have lower high school completion rates than either whites or blacks, a trend that dates back to the early 1970s. The high school completion rate for Hispanics aged 18 to 24 in 1998 was only 63 percent, compared with 90 percent for whites and 81 percent for blacks.

- Health: Hispanic children are less likely to have health insurance than either white or black children. In 1998, 70 percent of Hispanic children were covered by health insurance, compared with 96 percent of white and 80 percent of black children.

- Family structure: Hispanic women now have the highest rate of out-of-wedlock births. In 1998, there were 90 out-of-wedlock births for every 1,000 unmarried Hispanic women aged 15 to 44. This rate was compared with 38 births for every 1,000 unmarried white women and 73 for every 1,000 unmarried black women.

- Poverty: Hispanic children are more likely than either black or white children to be poor. They also are more likely to live in very poor neighborhoods, which often offer less social support to families raising children. In 1997, 61 percent of poor Hispanic children lived in neighborhoods with a high concentration of poor residents (more than 40 percent in poverty), compared with 56 percent of poor white children and 53 percent of poor black children.

- Teenage childbearing: Hispanic young women are more likely to become teenage parents than either their white or black counterparts. In 1996, the teenage birth rate was 177.8 for every 1,000 Hispanic females aged 15 to 19, compared with 68.1 per 1,000 for whites and 157.1 per 1,000 for blacks.

- Youth suicide: Hispanic youth are more likely to report they have considered or attempted suicide. In 1999, 20 percent of Hispanic youth reported they had considered suicide, compared with 15 percent of black youth and 18 percent of white youth. Thirteen percent of Hispanic youth attempted suicide that year, compared with 7 percent of white and black youth.

In tracking the data on children, youth, and families, we also identified positive markers within the Hispanic population that warrant equal attention. For example, Hispanics outperformed blacks and whites on three measures of a healthy start to life. In 1998, Hispanics had:

- the lowest infant mortality rate (6 deaths per 1,000 live births, compared with 14 for blacks and 6 for whites);

- the lowest percentage of low-birth-weight babies (6 percent, compared with 13 percent for blacks and 7 percent for whites); and

- the lowest percentage of births to women who smoked during pregnancy (4 percent, compared with 10 percent for blacks and 16 percent for whites).

What's more, Hispanic women have made great strides in getting prenatal care. The percentage of Hispanic women receiving early prenatal care jumped from 60 percent in 1980 to 74 percent in 1998, reflecting similar improvements on this measure by white and black women.

This bad news/good news picture of conditions affecting Hispanic families and children is just one part of a larger picture of the Hispanic population at the beginning of this new century. It is a population that represents a rich mix of nationalities, embracing those with roots in Cuba, Mexico, Puerto Rico, Spain, and countries throughout Central and South America. It is a population that includes people whose families have lived in the United States for several generations and those who have just arrived. It is a population that includes those who struggle to read and write--in any language—as well as graduates of prestigious universities. With Hispanics, as with all ethnic groups, there is a profusion of variations.

Data can help us to identify and understand these variations. Most important, from a policy perspective, data can help us pinpoint where there are unmet needs within this large and diverse population so we can target our responses to these needs more effectively.

Take the statistics on high school completion rates. They suggest many Hispanic youth and young adults will be less prepared than their white and black peers to enter or progress in the labor force.

For too long, we have cast social policy almost exclusively in terms of black-white relations.

Or, consider the statistics on youth suicide. They ought to raise questions about the causes of such despair and the availability of mental health or other services in Hispanic communities to combat it.

Consider the statistics on the teenage birth rate. They serve as a reminder of the need to couch campaigns to combat teenage pregnancy in language and action that is culturally sensitive, as well as to examine the special vulnerabilities in the lives of Hispanic youth. Or look at the statistics on health insurance coverage for Hispanic families. In the case of low-income families, they suggest many Hispanics are unaware of the availability of the Children's Health Insurance Program and other services for which they might be eligible.

For too long, we have cast social policy almost exclusively in terms of black-white relations. The Census 2000 numbers documenting the explosive growth of the Hispanic population are a wake-up call to widen our focus. And part of this involves paying attention—really paying attention—to the children and families behind the numbers.

Figure 4
Census Statistics on Fluency in English

A	B	C
CA	10.66%	3,261,020
TX	8.26%	1,545,121
AZ	6.49%	302,126
NY	6.29%	1,079,854
NJ	5.37%	411,455
FL	5.18%	759,654
HI	4.81%	52,898
NV	4.64%	85,006
IL	4.58%	514,585
RI	4.51%	42,762
NM	4.22%	69,790
US	**4.13%**	**10,513,832**
MA	4.05%	232,191
DC	3.53%	17,890
CO	3.47%	135,086
WA	3.03%	163,347
CT	2.92%	89,791
OR	2.86%	89,222
GA	2.45%	180,703
UT	2.36%	46,931
MD	2.22%	106,961
NC	2.19%	158,769
ID	2.14%	25,182
NE	2.06%	31,800
VA	1.97%	125,451
MN	1.80%	80,041
AK	1.74%	9,838
IA	1.66%	43,819
DE	1.58%	11,219
OK	1.53%	47,800
PA	1.42%	158,093
SC	1.35%	48,826
WI	1.33%	64,906
MI	1.17%	105,067
TN	1.10%	57,124
LA	1.03%	41,441
IN	1.02%	55,929
AR	0.89%	21,476
MO	0.87%	43,849
KS	0.85%	20,578
AL	0.82%	33,114
OH	0.77%	78,991
NH	0.71%	7,931
SD	0.70%	4,729
WY	0.57%	2,572
KY	0.54%	19,904
VT	0.52%	2,903
ND	0.50%	2,933
ME	0.44%	5,131
MT	0.44%	3,646
MS	0.41%	10,483
WV	0.24%	3,975

A= Location
B= % Can't Speak English Well or at All
C= # Can't Speak English Well or at All

Source: U.S. Census Bureau

Hispanic Catholics

"El futuro" Is Here[3]

By Timothy Matovina
Commonweal, September 14, 2001

The parishioners of Saint Leander's Church in Northern California were in conflict. As the date approached for the feast of Our Lady of Guadalupe, the revered patroness of the Mexican people, a threat that the annual parish Guadalupe celebration would be canceled loomed. That year, the December 12 feast fell on the third Sunday of Advent. Because the Sunday Mass takes precedence over feast days, the parish liturgical director had declared that no Mass for Guadalupe could be celebrated. But congregants of Hispanic descent were distraught and bewildered. How, they wondered, could a Catholic parish fail to offer their celestial mother proper honor on her feast day? After further consternation and discussion, however, the pastoral staff agreed to a compromise. A Mass in honor of Guadalupe would be celebrated at 5 a.m., early enough so as not to upset the regular Sunday Mass schedule. "How many would come at such an early hour anyway?" pastoral leaders reasoned. To their amazement, despite the cold, dark winter morning, by the time the Mass began a standing-room-only assembly had gathered to acclaim their patroness and fulfill their long-standing sacred tradition.

Such instances of misunderstanding, disagreement, and at times even open conflict are not uncommon as the Hispanic presence in U.S. Catholicism continues to expand rapidly. Of course, not all Hispanics are newcomers to the United States; in fact, Hispanic Catholics have lived in what is now the United States twice as long as the nation has existed. Subjects of the Spanish crown founded the first diocese in the "New World" at San Juan, Puerto Rico, in 1513 and, at Saint Augustine, Florida, in 1565, the first permanent European settlement in what is now the continental United States. But despite their long-standing presence, for much of U.S. history, Hispanics have constituted a relatively small and frequently overlooked group within U.S. Catholicism.

In the last half-century, however, the number and influence of Hispanics in the United States have increased dramatically. An influx of newcomers from such diverse locales as Puerto Rico, Cuba,

---

the Dominican Republic, El Salvador, Guatemala, Nicaragua, Colombia, Peru, Ecuador, and Argentina, along with ongoing Mexican immigration, has added to the ranks of an established Hispanic population composed primarily of Catholics of Mexican descent. More important, Hispanic Catholic communities, previously concentrated in New York, the Southwest, and some Midwestern cities, now extend from Seattle to Boston, from Miami to Alaska. The 2000 census revealed that Latinos in the United States number some 35.3 million, 12.5 percent of the total population, and that they now compose the largest minority group in the country. Today, Hispanics are also the largest ethnic group within U.S. Catholicism; in the first decades of the new century, they will make up the majority of U.S. Catholics.

Hispanics are also the largest ethnic group within U.S. Catholicism.

An expanding Hispanic presence is part of larger demographic shifts within U.S. Catholicism. A century ago, the U.S. Catholic Church was an overwhelmingly immigrant church of Northern and Southern Europeans. Today, the church, largely run by middle-class Catholics, descendants of those immigrants, has growing numbers of Hispanic, Asian, and African immigrants, along with sizable contingents of U.S.-born Latinos, African Americans, and some Native Americans.

In response to the increasing Hispanic presence, a number of English-speaking Catholics have made considerable efforts to work with their Latino co-religionists and offer them a sense of welcome. Particularly in the decades since Vatican II, women religious, clergy, and lay leaders at the national, regional, diocesan, and parish levels have invested significant amounts of time and material resources to help develop and expand ministries with Latino Catholics. On the national level, the Hispanic-led Encuentro 2000 held in Los Angeles, which gathered more than five thousand leaders from the diverse racial and ethnic groups in U.S. Catholicism, clearly illustrates recent ministerial efforts by and with Latinos. At present the twenty-six Hispanic bishops compose 7 percent of the U.S. hierarchy; approximately 80 percent of all dioceses and 20 percent of all parishes engage in ministry with Hispanics. These developments, which encompass initiatives to increase Spanish-language Masses, evangelization efforts, renewal movements, and feast-day celebrations, are visible signs that Catholicism in the United States is responding to this seismic shift in its demographic profile.

Despite the good intentions these success stories demonstrate, an alarming number of Hispanic Catholics feel alienated, rejected, and dissatisfied with Catholicism in the United States. One clear indication of these sentiments is Andrew Greeley's widely cited sociological research, which shows that some sixty thousand U.S. Hispanics "defect" from their ancestral religion every year—nearly 1 million since 1973. Most of these Latinos who have left Roman Catholicism have embraced Protestantism, especially in its Pentecostal and evangelical forms.

> *Some sixty thousand U.S. Hispanics "defect" from their ancestral religion every year.*

Analysis of the seeming disparity between increased Hispanic Catholic ministerial initiatives and the loss of Hispanic Catholics is varied. Many observers agree, however, that in contrast to most Catholic parishes, relatively small Protestant congregations are attractive because they provide a stronger sense of family and fellowship, a strict moral code based on clear biblical principles, a pronounced orientation toward mission, more indigenous Spanish-speaking pastors, and worship services in which Latinos can pray in their own language and cultural style.

It is not yet clear whether these Hispanic converts will persist in Pentecostal and other groups. Initial studies indicate that some Latinos maintain dual or even multiple denominational attachments; thus they may attend a Protestant congregation regularly for Sunday worship but celebrate baptisms, funerals, and other events in a Catholic parish. Other Hispanics in the United States follow the path of religious seekers; once they have left Catholicism their propensity for changing congregations or denominations again increases significantly. And some Hispanics do return to the Catholic fold, such as Mary Navarro Farr of San Antonio. After eight years in an evangelical church, Navarro Farr became upset with the anti-Catholicism in her congregation and was drawn back to a Catholic parish by "the treasure of the Eucharist, the maternal care of Our Lady of Guadalupe, and the music and sacred imagery" she remembered from her childhood. Despite such examples, there is no sign that the Hispanic leakage from Catholic ranks will abate in the proximate future.

To be sure, a number of Catholic parishes create hospitable environments in which Latinos experience a sense of familiarity and welcome that is similar to that offered in Protestant congregations. However, many analysts overlook a crucial difference experienced by Latinos in these two branches of Christianity: in Catholic communities, Hispanics may feel a sense of welcome, but in more autonomous Protestant congregations, particularly those of the Pentecostals and evangelicals, they are usually in charge. Intentionally or not, Euro-American Catholics who welcome their Hispanic sisters and brothers and practice "cultural sensitivity" frequently embody the subtle (and sometimes not-so-subtle) message that Latinos are guests and that English-speaking Catholics are the owners of the house. While hospitality and "cultural sensitivity" are an essential first step in ministry with Hispanics, often implicit is the notion that those in power will remain in power. At best, Hispanic traditions and religious expressions will be tolerated, but the established group will control and limit the conditions of this pluralism and diversity. For example, when Hispanics attempt to make a parish feel more like home by placing one of their own sacred images in the worship space or scheduling a Spanish Mass in a "prime-time" slot on Sunday morning, established parishioners frequently rebuff them with the claim that "our ancestors built this church" or "we were here first." If Hispanics challenge such a response, their Euro-American co-religionists often perceive them as being unappreciative of the welcome offered them.

> *The difference between receiving hospitality and feeling at home is not a new issue.*

The difference between receiving hospitality and feeling at home is not a new issue in U.S. Catholicism. European immigrant groups such as the Germans, Poles, Italians, Slovaks, Czechs, and Ukrainians, among others, staked out their own turf and created "national parishes." But the strategy of building ethnic enclave parishes has long since been abandoned in the United States. Latino Catholic leaders like Jesuit Allan Figueroa Deck bemoan this fact, noting that the national parish was a "fabulously successful approach to the pastoral care of immigrants for more than a hundred years." Still, Figueroa Deck and other Hispanic leaders conclude that in contemporary U.S. Catholicism national parishes are "not, practically speaking, viable for a host of reasons," especially the declining number of priests and the fiscal strain caused by abandoned inner-city national parishes of previous European immigrant groups.

In light of the impracticality of national parishes for Hispanics, many pastoral leaders assume that Hispanics will participate in existing parishes and assimilate into U.S. church and society. Indeed, as with European immigrants, a number of Hispanic Catholics learn English, move to the middle class and mainstream U.S. society, and, in many cases, subsequently practice their faith in more heterogeneous, English-speaking parishes. But unlike European immigration, which dwindled to a mere trickle after the enactment of restrictive U.S. immigration laws in the early 1920s, Hispanic immigration shows no sign of diminishing. Such factors as ongoing immigration, more consistent contact with their homeland than European emigres who crossed the ocean, the tendency of Latinos to live in urban clusters, and their own efforts to retain their language and culture ensure that the Spanish tongue and Hispanic faith expressions will persist in U.S. Catholicism for the foreseeable future.

Thus U.S. Hispanic Catholicism finds itself in a precarious position. Hispanic Catholics look to their church leaders to support and accompany them in their struggles, faith development, and religious traditions, but at the same time many sense that the institutional infrastructure for Hispanic ministry lags farther behind. The shortfall of Hispanic clergy in particular poses a formidable obstacle in meeting the pastoral challenge. While various European immigrant groups suffered from a shortage of compatriot priests who identified with their customs, spoke their language, and represented their interests within the structures of U.S. Catholicism, none of these groups experienced a dearth of native clergy to the same extent as today's Hispanics.

Hispanic women have been consistently the primary transmitters of the faith.

Explanations for the lack of Hispanic vocations to the priesthood are varied, but many Latino leaders point to a history of scant educational opportunities, ethnic prejudice and outright discrimination in seminaries, strong kinship ties among Hispanics that deter prospective candidates from leaving the family circle, and cultural norms that conflict with the requirement of mandatory celibacy. Moreover, as sociologist of religion Ana Maria Diaz-Stevens argues, Latino Catholicism has a "matriarchal core." With the historic lack of indigenous Latino priests, Hispanic women have been consistently the primary transmitters of the faith and exercised autonomous authority in the devotional life of their people. While this matriarchal core continues to shape Latino Catholicism, enabling it to retain a formative role in Hispanic families and communities, the lack of Latino clergy gives Hispanics decidedly less access to decision-making processes in a church with a male hierarchy.

Of course, many Latinos populate territorial parishes that in effect are national parishes, since their congregations are overwhelmingly Hispanic. Not surprisingly, a number of Hispanics, especially recent immigrants, feel at home in these parishes. Similarly, Latino initiatives to establish or support diocesan Hispanic ministry offices, parish organizations, feast-day celebrations, and devotional practices help Hispanics create a home within the structures of U.S. Catholicism. The incident at Saint Leander's in California, in which persistent Hispanic devotees organized and celebrated the traditional

Guadalupe feast at their parish, illustrates this point well. Such initiatives offer some hope that Latinas and Latinos will participate increasingly in the life, faith, and leadership structures of U.S. Catholic parishes and dioceses.

The progression from hospitality to homecoming, so ably met by the national parishes for previous generations of European immigrants, remains a challenge at the heart of the future of U.S. Catholicism. Like those European immigrants who sacrificed their time, energy, and scarce material resources to build and support their own national parishes, Latinos seek a sense of ownership in their parishes, worship, pious societies, and the wider church. In their pastoral letter on Hispanic ministry (1983) and their national pastoral plan for Hispanic ministry (1987), the U.S. Catholic bishops called for more widespread and effective ministry among Hispanics. But, as many bishops themselves observe, the issue is not so much one of pastoral vision and strategy as of implementation. There is no simple formula for pastoral responses applicable to all situations and communities. Concrete implementation strategies range from incorporating Hispanic religious traditions and sacred iconography into the worship life of local communities to fostering greater parity among Latinos and other leadership groups at all levels within the church. Each local context requires creative action that enables parish and diocesan leaders to promote a sense of belonging and ownership among Latinas and Latinos. Only in this way will the Catholic Church in the United States achieve another major step in the long process to forge a viable, vital Catholic community in a pluralistic church and society.

Figure 5

Population by Race and Hispanic Origin for the United States: 2000

Race and Hispanic or Latino	Number	Percent of total population
RACE		
Total population	**281,421,906**	**100.0**
One race	274,595,678	97.6
White	211,460,626	75.1
Black or African American	34,658,190	12.3
American Indian and Alaska Native	2,475,956	0.9
Asian...	10,242,998	3.6
Native Hawaiian and Other Pacific Islander	398,835	0.1
Some other race................................	15,359,073	5.5
Two or more races...............................	6,826,228	2.4
HISPANIC OR LATINO		
Total population	**281,421,906**	**100.0**
Hispanic or Latino	35,305,818	12.5
Not Hispanic or Latino............................	246,116,088	87.5

Source: U.S. Census Bureau, Census 2000 Redistricting (Public Law 94-171) Summary File, Tables PL1 and PL2.

Figure 6

Reproduction of Questions on Race and Hispanic Origin From Census 2000

→ NOTE: Please answer BOTH Questions 5 and 6.

5. Is this person Spanish/Hispanic/Latino? Mark ☒ the "No" box if not Spanish/Hispanic/Latino.
   - ☐ No, not Spanish/Hispanic/Latino
   - ☐ Yes, Mexican, Mexican Am., Chicano
   - ☐ Yes, other Spanish/Hispanic/Latino — Print group. ↗
   - ☐ Yes, Puerto Rican
   - ☐ Yes, Cuban

6. What is this person's race? Mark ☒ one or more races to indicate what this person considers himself/herself to be.
   - ☐ White
   - ☐ Black, African Am., or Negro
   - ☐ American Indian or Alaska Native — Print name of enrolled or principal tribe. ↗

   - ☐ Asian Indian
   - ☐ Chinese
   - ☐ Filipino
   - ☐ Japanese
   - ☐ Korean
   - ☐ Vietnamese
   - ☐ Other Asian — Print race. ↗
   - ☐ Native Hawaiian
   - ☐ Guamanian or Chamorro
   - ☐ Samoan
   - ☐ Other Pacific Islander — Print race. ↗

   - ☐ Some other race — Print race. ↗

Source: U.S. Census Bureau, Census 2000 questionnaire.

Figure 7

Percentage of Minority Population per State 2000

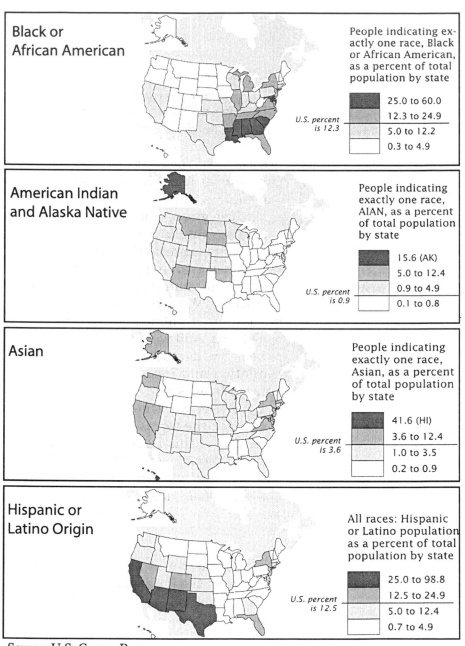

Source: U.S. Census Bureau

American Diversity and the 2000 Census[4]

By Nathan Glazer
The Public Interest, Summer 2001

The 2000 census, on which the Census Bureau started issuing reports in March and April of 2001, reflected, in its structure and its results, the two enduring themes of American racial and ethnic diversity, present since the origins of American society in the English colonies of the Atlantic coast: first, the continued presence of what appears to be an almost permanent lower caste composed of the black race; and second, the ongoing process of immigration of races and peoples from all quarters of the globe, who seem, within a few generations, to merge into a common American people.

To make two such large generalizations is admittedly a bold move. Undoubtedly, as further data from the census is released, we will have evidence of the continuing progress of American blacks in education, occupational diversity, and income. We will have grounds for arguing that the effects of integration into a common people can be seen, at long last, among American blacks. And when it comes to the new waves of immigration of the past few decades, some will question whether the process of assimilation and incorporation, which has swallowed up so many groups and races and religions into a common American people, will continue to work its effects on the new groups now gathered together under the terms "Hispanic" and "Asian." Yet I believe it can be argued that this large distinction in the processes of assimilation and integration that has persisted during the three- or four-century history of American diversity—the distinction between blacks and others—still shows itself, and still poses some of the most difficult questions for American society.

The First Census

The distinction makes itself evident in the very history and structure of the census, and in the character of the data that it first presents to the public today. In the first census of 1790, required for purposes of apportionment by the U.S. Constitution adopted in 1787, the separation between blacks and whites was already made. Indeed, that separation was itself foreshadowed by the Constitu-

4. Reprinted with permission of the author from *The Public Interest*, No. 144 (Summer 2001), pp. 3–18. Copyright © 2001 by National Affairs, Inc.

tion, which, in a famous compromise, decreed that "Representatives . . . shall be apportioned among the several states . . . according to their respective numbers, which shall be determined by adding to the whole number of free persons . . . three-fifths of all other persons." Those "other persons" were slaves. The "three-fifths" was a compromise between excluding all slaves for purposes of apportionment (which would have reduced the weight of the Southern slave states in the union) or counting them simply as persons (which would have given the slave states too great weight).

The census could have fulfilled the requirements of the Constitution by counting only slaves. But what was to be done with free blacks? There were, even then, free blacks, but their civil status was sharply below that of whites. It was apparently decided that they could not be simply numbered among the "free persons" referred to in the Constitution but had to be clearly distinguished from whites. So the first census went beyond the Constitution: It counted "free white males and females" as one category, "slaves" as another, but then added a category of "all other free persons." The count of "other persons"—slaves—and "all other free persons"—free blacks—produced the total number of blacks. Thus from the beginning, white could be differentiated from black. That has remained the most enduring distinction in the U.S. census.

In that first census, following the apportionment provision of the Constitution, "Indians not taxed" were also excluded. Over time, this simple scheme has been extended to cover other races and ethnic groups as they entered the new nation through immigration, to a degree which is possibly unique among national censuses, and which we will explore below. But the census begins crucially with the distinction between white and black. As Clara Rodriguez writes in her book *Changing Race*:

> Between the drafting of the Constitution of 1787 and the taking of the first census in 1790, the term white became an explicit part of [the free population]. . . . Theoretically, those in political charge could have chosen another definition for the [free population]. . . . They could have chosen "free English-speaking males over sixteen" or "free males of Christian descent" or "of European descent." But they chose color. Having named the central category "white" gave a centrality and power to color that has continued throughout the history of the census.

But of course this reflected the centrality of the black-white distinction in American society and the American mind. Rodriguez goes on to note that on occasion in the pre-Civil War censuses "aliens and foreigners not naturalized," separately numbered, are combined in one table with native whites and citizens in a table of "total white." "In the 1850 census, the category 'free whites' is changed to simply 'whites,' which suggests by this time it was evident that all the people in this category were free."

The Color Line

Color—race—has since been elaborated to a remarkable degree in the U.S. census. The most striking aspect of the American census of 2000—as of the few before—is that the short form, which goes to all American households, consists mostly of questions on race and "Hispanicity." Two large questions ask for the respondent's race, and whether the respondent is of "Spanish/Hispanic" origin, and both go into considerable detail in trying to determine just what race, and just what kind of "Hispanic," the respondent is. The race question lists many possibilities to choose from, including, to begin with, "white" and "black," and going on to "Indian (Amer.)," with an addi-

---

Color—race—has since been elaborated to a remarkable degree in the U.S. census.

---

tional request to list the name of the tribe, "Eskimo," or "Aleut." And then under the general heading "Asian or Pacific Islander (API)," it lists as separate choices Chinese, Filipino, Hawaiian, Korean, Vietnamese, Japanese, Asian Indian, Samoan, Guamanian, "Other API," and finally "Other race (print name)." In the 2000 census, it was possible for the first time for the respondent to check more than one race. This change was made after an extended discussion in the 1990s about how to account for those with parents of different race, who wanted to check off both, or perhaps more than two.

The question on whether one is Spanish/Hispanic also goes on to list a range of possibilities: "Mexican, Mexican-Am. [for "American"], or Chicano" (to account for the fact that Mexican Americans choose different terms to describe themselves), "Puerto Rican," "Cuban," and "other Spanish/Hispanic," with again the request to write in one group. In the 1990 census, a host of examples—"Argentinean, Colombian, Dominican, Nicaraguan, Salvadoran, Spaniard, and so on," was offered.

The observant and conscientious citizen may note that many other matters of interest to the census and the polity—whether one is of foreign birth or not, a citizen or not, and one's education, occupation, income, housing status, etc.—are all relegated to the long form, which goes to a large sample of citizens. And he may also ask why the census pays such great and meticulous attention to race and ethnicity (or rather one kind of ethnicity, that of Spanish-Hispanic background).

Many answers, going back to the first census of 1790, and before that, to the Constitution that prescribed a regular decennial census, and before that, to the first arrival of black slaves in the English colonies in the early seventeenth century, are available to explain why the first statistics the census makes available today, along with the raw number of the population in each state and locality, are those describing race and ethnicity. But there is also an immediate and proximate answer of much more recent currency: Congress requires that ethnic and racial statistics be available within a year of the census for the purpose of redrawing the boundaries of congressional districts, and the other electoral districts for state legislative assemblies, and for city and county elected officials.

The course of the law has been to use statistical tests to determine whether there is discrimination.

Ethnic and racial statistics have become so significant for redistricting because of the Civil Rights Act of 1964, the Voting Rights Acts of 1965, and the latter's amendments of 1970, 1975, and 1982. Admittedly, these acts, which simply proscribe discrimination on the basis of race and national background, did not necessarily require such detailed statistics to check on the presence of discrimination in various spheres of life and, in particular, in the free exercise and effect of the vote. But the course of the law has been to use statistical tests to determine whether there is discrimination. The right enshrined in the Voting Rights statute, to the free exercise of the vote, has been extended through litigation and administrative and judicial rule-making to cover rights to the drawing of congressional and other district boundaries in such a way as to protect or enhance the ability of minority groups, blacks in particular, but others too, to elect representatives of their own group. If blacks are to be protected from discrimination, interpreted as the creation of voting districts that enhance the power of blacks to choose a black representative, if they are so inclined, then detailed statistics of how a race is distributed are necessary.

That is why the first statistics that come out of the census are those that make it possible to redraw district lines immediately on the basis of the new census, and for various groups to challenge the new district lines if they are aggrieved. "Growing minority groups will likely face lawsuits over redistricting," reads one news headline in the *Wall Street Journal*, with the subtitle, "One California assemblyman says his caucus 'will sue' regardless of the rationale for redrawing districts." The story tells us:

> Here in Orange County [California], . . . a dozen Latino officials last week huddled in a spartan conference room over a map of Southern California as Art Montez, felt-tipped marker in hand, lopped the city of Westminster off the state's 68th Assembly

District. Westminster's large population of conservative whites makes it "Impossible for a minority candidate to win there," Mr. Montez, a political activist and school board member, explained to the group.

But this is only the beginning of a struggle that will move through the state legislature and almost inevitably to the Department of Justice and the Federal courts, where the racial and ethnic statistics and the role they have played in drawing up new districts will be carefully examined and disputed. For those with the responsibility of drawing up the new districts—the state legislatures primarily—the central concern is generally the maximization of the number of representatives of the party in power in the state legislature. A second concern is to maintain for the incumbents of the favored party district boundaries that secure their return. But overlaying these historic political reasons for drawing district lines, which courts accept in some measure as legitimate, is a new imperative, the protection of minority groups.

Racial and ethnic statistics and the role they have played in drawing up new districts will be carefully examined.

The Four "Official" Minorities

"Portrait of a Nation" is the title of a major story on the first results of the census in the *New York Times*, and it is accompanied by elaborate colored maps. The colors provide information on the distribution of the minority population—blacks, Hispanics, Asians, American Indians.

To explain how these have become the American minorities—to the exclusion of many other possible minorities—and why their numbers and distribution are in every newspaper report considered the most important information to look for in the census, would require a precis of American history. It is hardly necessary to explain why blacks are the first of the minority groups. They have been a significant presence in the United States and its predecessor colonies from the beginning. Our greatest national trauma—the Civil War—was directly occasioned by the problem of black slavery, and the most significant amendments to the Constitution became part of that quasi-sacred document in order to deal with the consequences of black slavery.

American Indians were there even before the beginning but were considered outside the society and polity unless they individually entered into non-Indian-American society, as many have, through intermarriage and assimilation. Their status has changed over time, from outside the polity as semi-sovereign foreign nations, to subjects almost without rights, to a population confined on reservations, to one that now increasingly becomes part of the society.

Indeed, today, to be able to claim an American-Indian heritage is a plus for one's social status. This is too complex a history to be reviewed here. There is good reason to maintain a separate count of Indians, though there are great complexities in doing so.

"Hispanics," too, were there from before the beginning, if we take into account the Spaniards and Creoles moving up from Mexico who had already established colonial settlements in northern Mexico— what is now the Southwest of the United States—before the first English colonists had established permanent settlements on the Atlantic coast. Of course, they were not "Hispanics" then. Two hundred and fifty years later, this mixed population became part of the United States as a result of the annexation of the northern part of Mexico after the Mexican-American War. But it contained then a small population of Mexicans and Indians, and interestingly enough, despite the sense of racial difference felt by the Anglo-Americans, and despite the prejudice against Mexicans, they were not differentiated in the census as a separate group until 1930. Until then, one presumes, they were "white." In that year, Clara Rodriguez notes, a census publication, responding to the increase in immigration from Mexico as a result of the revolutionary wars and troubles of the 1920s, reported that "persons of Mexican birth or parentage who were not definitely reported as white or Indian were designated Mexican" and included in "other races." In 1940, this policy was changed, and Mexicans became white again. By 1950, added to the growing number of Mexicans in the Southwest, as a result of immigration in the previous decades, was a large number of Puerto Ricans in New York City, migrants from the island of Puerto Rico, which had been annexed after the Spanish-American War of 1898. In that census year, the two were combined in the census—along with smaller numbers of other groups—into a "Spanish-surnamed" group.

In the wake of Castro's victory in Cuba, a third large group of Latin Americans emigrated to the United States. Whether or not one could make a single meaningful category out of Mexicans, Puerto Ricans, and Cubans, separated as they are by culture, history, and to some extent by racial characteristics, they were so combined, with a host of other Spanish-speaking groups, into a "Hispanic" category in the census of 1970. The creation of the category was a response to political pressure from Mexican Americans. It now includes large numbers of Nicaraguans, Guatemalans, Salvadorans, Dominicans, Colombians, Ecuadorians, and others fleeing the political and economic troubles of their homelands.

Racial and ethnic groups are conventionally described today as "constructed," but it is worth noting that this "construction" is not simply the result of white determinations—it is also the result of group insistence, at least to some degree. As Peter Skerry tells us in his book *Counting on the Census*:

> The finalized questionnaires for the 1970 census were already at the printers when a Mexican American member of the U.S. Interagency Committee on Mexican American affairs demanded that a specific Hispanic-origin question be included. . . . Over the opposition of Census Bureau officials, who argued against inclusion of an untested question so late in the process, [President] Nixon ordered the secretary of commerce and the census director to add the question.

And so "Hispanics" were born. The pressure to maintain the category, with all its subdistinctions, persists. The distinguished demographer Stanley Lieberson has written about a well-intentioned intervention at a conference preparatory to the 1990 census:

> I naively suggested that there was no reason to have an Hispanic question separate from the ethnic ancestry question [an ancestry question has been part of the long form since 1980] since the former . . . could be classified as a subpart of the latter. Several participants from prominent Hispanic organizations were furious at such a proposal. They were furious, by the way, not at me (just a naive academic), rather it was in the form of a warning to census personnel of the consequences that would follow were this proposal to be taken seriously.

The last of the four minorities distinguished in the census is the "Asian," a creation—or construction—that has as complex a history as that of the Hispanic. Chinese and Japanese individuals were undoubtedly present in the United States before they were first listed as "races" in 1870—by then there was a substantial population of Chinese in California, and they were already the subject of racist legislation. In 1930, "Filipino," "Hindu" [sic], and "Korean" were added as separate races, and it became the pattern to add a new "race" for each Asian immigrant group as it became numerous. Eventually, we have the complex category of "Asian and Pacific Islander" (API), with all its listed subgroups.

As in the case of the Mexicans, the initial discrimination that made each of these a separate group was undoubtedly racist and reflected a sense of white superiority. The Asian groups were all subjected to discriminatory legislation. One could be naturalized as a citizen only if one were "white" (or, after the Civil War, black). All sorts of restrictions, from land ownership to the pursuit of certain professions or occupations, were imposed on them by various states because they were noncitizens. But Asian immigrants were denied because of race the right of becoming citizens. These groups were indeed nonwhite, but their separate classification was more than a matter of keeping neat statistics. An identity was being selected for a group felt to be inferior. This identity may well have been the one the members of the group would have chosen, but it was not they who decided they should be numbered aside from the dominant whites.

What has happened then to all those others once considered "minorities"?

In more recent decades, the power to name and describe has shifted: The groups themselves, or those who speak for them, now shape how they are to be described, named, differentiated, and counted. And the political and administrative process bends to their desires. Why do we distinguish so many subgroups among the "Asian and Pacific Islanders"? There is a separate story for each category. But note one account by Peter Skerry from the political history of the census: The Census Bureau tried to simplify and shorten the Asian and Pacific Islander question for the 1990 census. Congressman Robert Matsui introduced legislation "in which the formatting of the API race question was spelled out, even to the point of stipulating that 'Taiwanese' be one of the subgroups. . . . It was only President Reagan's pocket veto that blocked this extraordinary degree of Congressional involvement in what is ordinarily considered the technical side of questionnaire design."

A Melting Pot?

These then are the four "official" minorities, though no law names these and only these as minorities. But what has happened then to all those others once considered "minorities," ethnic groups that were in the first quarter of the twentieth century in the eye of public attention because of the recency of their immigration, their lower social and economic status, and the concern that they could not be assimilated? Immigration was largely cut off by law in the 1920s because of these concerns. The United States has been a country of immigration since its origins, and by some measures the immigration of the first two decades of the twentieth century was much greater than the immigration of the last three decades, which has swelled the numbers of the new minorities. Had one picked up a book on American minorities and race relations in the 1950s, Jews might have been presented as the typical minority: Much of the social theory and social psychology on minority status was formulated with the position of Jews in mind. Jews were a major element in the mass immigration that preceded the present one, from the 1880s to the 1920s. Other major components of this immigration were Italians, Poles, Hungarians, Czechs, Slovaks, Slovenes, Croats, Serbs, Greeks, Armenians, Lebanese, Syrians, and many other peoples of Eastern and Southern Europe and the Near East. Are they no longer included in the story of American minorities?

One can go further back and ask, what has happened to the Irish, the Germans, the Swedes, Norwegians, and Danes, and the host of immigrants who came earlier and were also once sharply distinguished as separate groups, different from the founding group, the English? Does not the story of American diversity include all these too? How has the palette become restricted to the four minorities that play so large a role in the current census?

> *Immigrants merge in two or three generations into a common American people.*

The simple answer is that integration and assimilation reduce over time the differences that distinguish one group from another, or from the original settler group, what Tocqueville called the "Anglo-Americans." We have no good term for this group. WASP ("White Anglo-Saxon Protestant") has been used in recent decades, ironically or derisively, for the founding element and their descendants. But aside from the necessity to distinguish such a group historically, no term is currently really necessary: Immigrants merge in two or three generations into a common American people, and ethnic distinctions become less and less meaningful. Ethnicity becomes symbolic, a matter of choice, to be noted on the basis of name or some other signifier on occasion, of little matter for most of one's life.

At one time, the census distinguished the foreign-born by place of birth, and the foreign-born parents of the native-born by place of birth, permitting us to track ethnic groups (somewhat uncertainly, owing to the lack of fit between ethnicity and national boundaries) for two generations. The rest of the population was classed as natives of native parentage, not further distinguishable, at least in the census, on the basis of their ethnicity. In 1980, the question on birthplace of parents was dropped, to the distress of sociologists and students of ethnicity. A new question on "ancestry" was added, which, in theory, would permit us to connect people to ethnic groups in the third generation and beyond. But the amount of mixture among groups, through marriage, is today such that the answers to the ancestry question, if one is not an immigrant or the child of an immigrant with a clear sense of ancestry, are not helpful in distinguishing an ethnic group much beyond the second generation. The answers then become so variable, so dependent on cues from the census itself—such as the examples the census form gives to the respondent regarding what is intended by the term "ancestry," which is by no means clear to many people—as to be hardly meaningful. It is a question that permits some 40 million Americans, seven times the population of Ireland, to declare that they are of "Irish" ancestry.

There are indeed differences of some significance based on ethnicity among the native white population, and sometimes these become evident—when home countries are involved in conflict, for example—or even paramount. This is particularly evident for Jews, who are marked not only as a religion (but the census rigorously refrains from asking any question or accepting any response on religion) but also by ethnicity (but to the census, Jews are not an ethnic group but a religion). The exceptional history that resulted in the killing of most of the Jews of Europe, and the creation of a regularly imperiled State of Israel, ties Jews to their past and to their co-religionists abroad much more than other ethnic groups. They are not to be found in any census count—they are not a "race" and not even, for the census, an "ancestry," even though that answer would make sense for most Jews.

Sociologists and political scientists can plumb for differences among the native white population, and they will find not insignificant differences in income, occupation, political orientation, and so on. Jews, for example, are exceptional among "whites" for their regular overwhelming support for Democrats. Indeed, the differences among native whites, ethnically distinguished, may be greater than those among the official minority groups or between any of them and the native white population. Yet from the point of view of public opinion and official notice, these differences are not significant. The ethnic groups of the great immigrations of the nineteenth and early twentieth century have sunk below the horizon of official attention. They have merged into the "white" population, become integrated and assimilated, and only emerge as a special interest on occasion, stimulated by a conflict or crisis involving the home country.

"Whiteness Theory"

Recently, this somewhat benign view of American history, one in which immigrant groups steadily assimilate to, and become part of, the common American people, has been challenged by historians who argue that this was a strictly limited process, available only to whites, and, further, that many of those who were eventually included as full Americans had to overcome a presumption that they were not "really" white. In other words, race is crucial, both at its beginning and, by implication, throughout American history, for full inclusion. To take one powerful and clear statement of this position:

The saga of European immigration has long been held up as proof of the openness of American society, the benign and absorptive powers of American capitalism, and the robust health of American democracy. "Ethnic inclusion," "ethnic mobility," and "ethnic assimilation" on the European model set the standard upon which "America," as an ideal, is presumed to work; they provide the normative experience against which others are measured. But this pretty story suddenly fades once one recognizes how crucial Europeans' racial status as "free white persons" was to their gaining entrance in the first place; how profoundly dependent their racial inclusion was upon the racial exclusion of others; how racially accented the native resistance was even to their inclusion for something over half a century. [Matthew Frye Jacobson, in *Whiteness of a Different Color*.]

The implication of this point of view is that the present minorities as commonly understood exist not only because of the recency of their immigration but primarily because of color: They are not white. Their ability to become full and equal participants in American society is thereby limited because of America's racist character.

The racist character of the past is clear, ... but there has been a striking and irreversible change.

But I believe these "whiteness theorists" are wrong. The racist character of the past is clear, and a degree of racism in the present is also evident, despite radical changes in public opinion and major changes in law and legal enforcement. But there has been a striking and irreversible change between the 1920s—when immigration from Eastern and Southern Europe was sharply reduced and immigration from Asia was banned entirely—and the postwar decades and, in particular, the period since the 1960s. Public institutions and significant private institutions today may only take account of race for the purpose of benefiting minorities.

The whiteness theorists may have a story to tell about the past, but it is one that has limited bearing on the present. The new immigrant groups are for the most part distinguished by race or quasi-racial characteristics from the population of European white origin. Yet it seems likely they progress pretty much at the same rate, affected by the same factors—their education and skills, their occupations, the areas of the country in which they settle, and the like—as the European immigrants of the past.

They merge into the common population at the same rate too. We will soon have analyses of marriages between persons of different race and ethnicity, to the extent the census makes possible, but we already know that the number and percentage of intermarriages between persons from the minorities and the majority has grown greatly in recent decades. One analysis of the 1990 census, reported by David T. Canon in his *Race, Redistricting, and Repre-*

sentation, shows that "for married people between the ages of twenty-five and thirty-four, 70 percent of Asian women and 39 percent of Hispanic women have white [sic] husbands." But only 2 percent of black women in the same age group were married to white men. The theme of black difference contrasted with the intermixture and merger of other groups is clearly sounded in these and other statistics.

The End of "Race"?

The first studies conducted by independent analysts of the 2000 census statistics brought up sharply the degree to which blacks are still distinguished from other minorities or subgroups in the United States by residential segregation. "Analysis of Census Finds Segregation Along With Diversity," reads one headline. "Segregation" in this analysis is measured by the diversity of census tracts, as experienced by the "average" person of a given group or race. The average white person lives in a tract that is 80 percent white, down from 85 percent in 1990; the average black person lives in a tract that is 51 percent black, down from 56 percent in 1990; the average Hispanic is less "segregated" by this measure—his tract is 45 percent Hispanic, and increased from 43 percent in 1990. But one may explain this degree of segregation and its rise since 1990 by the huge increase, based on immigration, much of it illegal, of the Hispanic population. The average Asian lives in a tract that is not particularly Asian—18 percent, as against 15 percent in 1990. This rise reflects to some degree the 50 percent increase of the Asian population, mostly through immigration, in the decade.

Local reporting focused on the relative proportions of the minority groups in each community, and also on the degree of segregation. Integration proceeds, but slowly. There are black census tracts in Boston with almost no whites and white tracts with almost no blacks. We calculate these figures every census, as if watching a fever report. The overall picture is that the segregation of blacks is great, the segregation of Hispanic groups, despite the recency of their immigration and their foreign tongue, is rather less, and little segregation is noted among Asians.

The big news of the census was that "Hispanics" had for the first time surpassed blacks in number, but that was only the case if one excluded from the black population those individuals who had chosen the race "black" along with another race. Hispanics rose to 35.3 million, a 61 percent increase in 10 years; blacks rose by about 16 percent to 34.7 million, or 36.4 million if one added those who chose more than one race. Blacks are 12.3 percent of the population, about the same percentage they have maintained for the past century. The increase in Hispanics was much greater than expected: It was gen-

erally agreed that one reason for this increase was a larger number
of illegal immigrants than had been previously calculated, 9 million according to one demographer instead of 7, perhaps as much
as 11 million according to another demographer.

Making the comparison between the two largest minorities was
complicated by the fact that respondents could choose more than
one race for the first time,
and 7 million did so. Analysis
of these mixed-race choices,
even reporting on them, is
not easy. A reporter writes:
"Five percent of blacks, 6
percent of Hispanics, 14 per-
cent of Asians and 2.5 percent of whites identified themselves as
multi-racial." But why are these multi-race choosers labeled
"black" or "Asian"? Is the "one drop" rule once used by the southern
states operating here? If someone chooses "American Indian" and
another race, do we include that person in the count of American
Indians? If we do, that would increase the number of American
Indians by more than 50 percent. The Office of Management and
Budget oversees the race and ethnic statistics compiled by federal
agencies, and it has determined that for their purposes (affirma-
tive-action monitoring and the like) all multi-race choosers who
chose white and a minority race are to be counted as being part of
the minority, a decision that has pleased minority advocates. But
does it reflect how these individuals see themselves?

> *It is clear many are eager
> to choose two or even more
> races.*

The mixed-race choices complicate the issue of choosing a base on
which to measure the progress of, or possible discrimination
against, minorities, an important step in affirmative action programs. That is the reason some minority leaders opposed allowing
the mixed-race option. If the base becomes smaller, the degree of
discrimination that one may claim in noting how many members of
the group have attained this or that position is reduced.

Now that the option exists, it is clear many are eager to choose
two or even more races. Among blacks there seems to be less willingness to choose two races than among Asians and American Indians—perhaps because it may be seen as something like race
betrayal. But it is noteworthy that younger persons more often
choose two races than older ones. If one creates a combined black
group by putting together blacks with those who choose black as
one of the races they check off, 2.3 percent of this combined group
50 years of age or older turn out to be multi-race choosers, but 8.1
percent of those 17 and younger choose more than one race. But
those who choose the option of black-white are still quite few—

fewer in number than those who choose white-other ("other" in the racial category means Hispanic), or white-Asian, or white-American Indian.

When the statistics of intermarriage are analyzed, one can be sure there will be a considerable rise in white-black marriages since 1990, even if the percentage of such intermarriages is considerably less than white-Asian or Hispanic-non-Hispanic marriages. Blacks are still more segregated, more separated, in residence than other minority groups. They are more sharply defined in their consciousness as separate: History has made them so. But even among blacks, one sees the process of assimilation and integration, as measured by choice of race and by intermarriage, at work. By the census of 2010 or 2020, these processes will be further advanced. Indeed, one may perhaps look forward to a time when our complex system of racial and ethnic counting is made so confusing by the number of possible choices, singular and multiple, that the whole scheme is abandoned. Many Americans hope so.

I Am What I Say I Am[5]

By Lise Funderburg
TIME, MARCH 26, 2001

According to Russell (my personal trainer by night, a lawyer by day, and a philosopher by disposition), I have white calves. Not white as in pasty, but as in Caucasian. My calves are—how to put it?—substantial, and their shape not only pegs me racially, Russell says, but also makes clear what kind of runner I would be (distance) if, say, hell were to freeze over and I were to take up that sport.

When I filled out my Census form last spring, the issue of my calves never came up. What did arise, however, was a new option that allowed Americans to claim identity in more than one racial group. When the result of this historic change was released last week, it showed that an unexpectedly large number of people had taken advantage of this choice: nearly 7 million, or 2.4% of the population. While the complexity of the outcome has sent demographers scrambling, I celebrate its promise.

Due to circumstances beyond my control (e.g., my birth), race is more plastic for me than for some. The catalog of purported racial characteristics I could assemble seems to be compounded rather than dissolved by my particular heritage: one black parent and one white. Examples follow.

My blackness: love of watermelon, fried foods and well-told stories that may not reside solely in the land of fact. Unconditional love for Stevie Wonder. Half-moons under my fingernails. Rhythm. A fondness for cities, for picking bones clean. A collectivist rather than colonialist view of the world. A behind of consequence. My father.

My whiteness: love of Joni Mitchell. A fondness for the Midwest. A taste for soy milk, vanilla flavored. Tendency to be underdressed at any event. Disdain for black-eyed peas. The ability to dwell, for long spells, in a world not eclipsed by race. Skin, eyes, hair. My mother.

Census 2000 didn't ask for these details, and unless I missed it, did not include an essay portion. But after years of research, the Census Bureau, by introducing its Check All That Apply option, did advance its stated belief that race is not a static concept. Critics of CATA see it variously as a threat to social justice in its perceived dilution of nonwhite constituencies, or as race obsessed, or as a flaccid nod to the burgeoning ranks of mixed-race Americans. But I think the Census people were savvy. Or, really, credit goes to their overseeing agency, the Office of Management and Budget, which is responsible for telling federal agencies how to use Census data in monitoring civil rights compliance. Now, when data are tabulated for a compliance issue, there is a simple formula. People who check a single race never move from their boxes; in situations where at least two boxes are checked, minority trumps white, and one minority will trump another, depending on the issue for which data are being collected. Sure, the formula is an embrace of the old one-drop rule (one drop of black blood makes you black), but this retrograde remedy is an appropriate answer to backward thinking, and what could be more backward than racism?

In my day-to-day life, it is thousands of unofficial, unsolicited enumerators who make the call on my race.

The CATA model has its flaws. Such a fundamental shift in how our country counts race will most likely have repercussions that are impossible to anticipate. And the numbers are indeed fuzzy. Many people—possibly 70% or more of African Americans, for example—could have checked more than one box but did not, for a host of reasons. Moreover, by asking people to self-identify, the Census Bureau's tabulations don't begin to measure the way race is typically assessed in our society. In my day-to-day life, it is thousands of unofficial, unsolicited enumerators who make the call on my race by way of offhand remarks, furtive glances, head wiggles, bullhorned street sermons, the pointed embrace, the casual snub, the kiss, the oversight, the intimacy, the job.

Despite its imperfections, the new census has taken a giant step toward recognizing that race is profoundly contextual, both in its origins and applications. "It's very clear that race is fluid, it's changing, it's dynamic," says Nampeo McKenney, who retired from the Census Bureau after a 40-year career that culminated in overseeing the CATA model. She means this in a global sense; I find it personally true from moment to moment. I can't stand the smell of chitterlings, but neither can my Aunt Ruthie, who won't allow them within a mile of her kitchen.

CATA transcends the peculiar racial quagmire in which this nation finds itself, a consequence of segregation and integration, hate and love, the personal squared off against the political. CATA is a pragmatic negotiation of a complicated social and political reality: namely, that the experience of race has broken out of traditional categories, while the experience of racism is still deeply rooted inside them.

Melting Pot or Salad Bowl?[6]

By Jo Ann S. Barefoot
ABA Banking Journal, September 2001

On May 5, President Bush did something no President had ever done before. He delivered his Saturday radio address in Spanish.

This came on the heels of reports on the 2000 census, which illustrate the profound changes underway in America's population. Growth rates for racial and ethnic minorities are dramatically outstripping increases in Americans of white European descent.

As these minority groups grow, potent forces will push them toward the traditional American melting pot. Meanwhile, a competing vision will seek to create a new American metaphor—a stew, or salad—to describe a new America where ethnic identities do not melt and meld, but instead remain distinctive.

For banks, such changes will generate new market opportunities—as well as new legal and regulatory risks—for banks throughout the country.

Who's up, who's down?

The census revealed important demographic patterns in many areas: aging, marriage, child-bearing, household formation, education, western migration, and more. Of special interest to banks, though, are shifts in the country's racial and ethnic makeup—the factors that drive fair-lending measurement and enforcement.

Summarizing these statistics is complicated by the fact that the 2000 census, for the first time, allowed people to check more than one box for race/ethnicity. No matter how you count, though, the results are important to consider:

- One in four Americans belongs to a minority group—up from one in five a decade ago. Minority populations skyrocketed 43%, to 86.9 million people, while the nation as a whole grew 13%, to a 281.4 million total.

- Hispanics have narrowly surpassed African-Americans to become the nation's largest minority group. They grew nearly 60% in 10 years, to 35 million people, representing 12.5% of the country's population.

6. Article by Jo Ann S. Barefoot from *ABA Banking Journal* September 2001. Copyright © American Bankers Association. Reprinted with permission.

- Asian-Americans' rank also grew rapidly. The number of people checking just the Asian census box grew by 48.3%, to 10.2 million. Added to people who checked both Asian-American and another box, the category rose by a whopping 72.2%—to 11.9 million.

- For the first time, non-Hispanic white Californians are a minority group in their state (which is home to one out of every eight Americans). They are now outnumbered by fast-growing ethnic populations, especially Hispanics and Asians.

- The multi-box counting system also produced a doubling in the numbers of people who are at least partly Native Americans and Alaska Natives, to about 4.1 million.

The new census numbers may throw a monkey wrench into America's political and regulatory machinery.

- The black population grew by 15.6% (one box checked) or 21.5% (multi-boxes), reaching 34.7 or 36.4 million, respectively.

- Non-Hispanic whites, while still the largest group at 194.6 million, grew only about 5%. Whites account for only 69% of the population—compared to 76% 10 years ago.

- Growing Hispanic and Asian populations sparked huge growth in big cities like New York. New York gained over 685,000 people, reaching nearly 8 million. Meanwhile, cities like Pittsburgh, populated largely by whites and African Americans, lost population. In New York, white residents declined 3.7%, while Hispanics grew by 30% and Asians by 52%–70%.

- Inter-racial or multi-ethnic families are growing fast. Nearly 7 million—2.4% of the total-checked multiple boxes on the census forms.

Given all this, it's perhaps not surprising that the city of Oakland, Calif., recently passed a rule requiring applicants for most city jobs to be proficient in at least two languages.

So, who, exactly, is a minority?

The new census numbers may throw a monkey wrench into America's political and regulatory machinery, because they reflect a pervasive breakdown in the race and ethnic categories that underlie numerous public policies and programs.

Bankers can ponder the Home Mortgage Disclosure Act data they submitted last time—all the numbers grouped so neatly along racial and ethnic lines—and then think about these new realities:

First, the seven million Americans who identified themselves as multi-racial apparently don't even reflect the true numbers. That's because those individuals who categorized themselves this way did so despite campaigns by civil-rights group urging them to list only their primary category.

The civil-rights advocates fear dilution of their political clout—for good reason. Current numbers of inter-racial couples are way up and preliminary numbers indicate the number of multi-racial children on this census was up to triple that of adults listed.

Second, the rising numbers of multi-ethnic individuals are making it hard to count and classify—or even to talk about—groupings of people. Before the 2000 census there was consideration of simply allowing people to check a box indicating that they were "multi-racial." This idea was fought successfully by minority interest groups, and replaced with the option to check more than one box.

One result is that the new data choices permitted 126 different racial combinations. Another result is the kind of tortured enumeration reflected in the above statistics—ethnic groups measured in ranges that include one-box-plus-multibox-checkers. In reality, however, a multi-box person who is three-quarters white Italian-American and one-quarter Japanese may not fit very logically in the same category as another who is three-quarters Pakistani and one quarter white.

Furthermore, even within single-group categories, more and more questions are being raised about what such numbers tell us. Take the Asian-American category. This covers people with roots in a wide range of countries. Chinese-Americans are still the largest group and grew fast—48%—to 2.4 million. Second-largest are Filipinos at 1.85 million. However, the fastest growing Asian segment is Indian—among both citizens and many resident knowledge-workers—whose numbers more than doubled to 1.7 million. Vietnamese increased 83%. These national origins, as well as Koreans, Japanese, Pakistanis, Cambodians, Malaysians and others, have very different genetic, cultural, and historical backgrounds. Similarly, the Hispanic grouping includes a vast range of kinds of people. They may come from over a dozen different countries in Latin America and the Caribbean, from Cuba to Peru to the two-thirds who are Mexican. They may also be Spaniards of entirely Caucasian descent. They include both the 60% of U.S. Hispanics who were born here and the 13 million who are immigrants.

Such differences are huge, as subgroups have vastly different profiles in terms of income levels; workforce participation; education; culture; and even politics. For instance, Mexican-Americans born in the U.S. graduate from high school at rates about equivalent to whites. Half of U.S.-born Hispanics in southern California own their own homes. According to a Latino National Political Survey in the mid-1990s, most Hispanics prefer to be identified by national origin like Salvadoran or Mexican, rather than lumped together under the Hispanic label.

The Hispanic label also spotlights the fact that census categories are an apples-and-oranges comparison because some focus on people descended from distinct races, and some don't. Critics question why one ethnic group—Hispanics—should be specially counted as if it were a race, which it is not. Why, they ask, don't we also track German- or Italian-Americans?

Politically, the answer seems to be that Hispanics are widely perceived as minorities vulnerable to discrimination who must therefore be counted in order to be protected. However, this logic leads to growing pressures from additional groups wanting to be treated as distinct minorities. Some Arab-Americans, for example, argue

---

The old system of classification and counting . . . increasingly resembles a square peg being pounded into a round hole.

---

that Moslems and people of Middle-Eastern descent are the targets of bias in our society.

Furthermore, the same logic calls into question why Asian-Americans need to be counted, given that they tend to have higher educational attainment than whites and that many Asian-American national groupings have higher incomes than whites. Also relevant, for banks, is the fact that HMDA data show Asian-Americans as less likely than whites to be denied mortgage credit.

These and other anomalies suggest that the old system of classification and counting—conceived in part to prevent discrimination on all sorts of fronts—increasingly resembles a square peg being pounded into a round hole.

Lessons for banks

When "minorities" aren't necessarily in the minority; when "racial" categories don't necessarily measure races; when "disadvantaged" groups have more education and income than advantaged ones; when millions of people perceive themselves to be—and are—so genetically mixed that they transcend any racial label; and when many Americans have less in common with those inside their "category" than with others outside it—then, it would seem, change must come.

Banks should prepare. But how?

1. Tap into the enormous opportunities embedded in minority markets.

Banks that want to grow have two choices: (a) they can fight for share in a static marketplace, or, (b) they can serve markets that are enjoying growth.

If you're looking for growth markets today—and ones with rising incomes—minority segments are a promising place to turn. This applies not just to border and coastal states, and not just to big cities. Globalization means that even small towns like Marysville, Ohio—home to a Honda plant that employs Japanese workers along with Americans—are increasingly linked to an international and multi-ethnic economic base.

Any bank in a high-technology area is likely serving a swelling population of Asians and Asian-Americans. A growing number of northern states, including New Jersey and Illinois, now have over a million Hispanics.

Banks should research these segments and figure out how best to attract, serve, and retain these customers. This means re-thinking everything, from product needs and marketing to branch locations and design of delivery channels to recruiting and training staff and offering multi-language services.

Making such efforts will not only fuel growth, but also limit the risk that fair-lending problems will surface because banks have stuck with traditional markets that, over time, become a shrinking part of the statistical base that regulators measure and monitor.

2. Prepare for a long period of chaos on the regulatory and legal fronts.

The demographic sea changes underway will force changes in public policy. For decades, racial groupings have been the bases for everything from drawing the boundaries of election districts, to set-asides for government contracts, to establishing two-tiered standards for hiring and in college admissions. And of course, they are the foundation of federal fair-lending enforcement and HMDA statistics.

A long-term battle will develop between those who believe this counting, and politics based on group identity, must continue, versus those who believe these should give way to race-blindness and individualism. Banking will likely be one of the battlegrounds in that war.

There will also be erosion of the mindset that assumes that powerful whites are routinely pitted against all minorities. Instead, minority groups will increasingly vie with one another for political power and economic advantages. Already, for instance, blacks and

Hispanics decry college selection standards that disproportionately admit Asian-Americans, who tend to score higher than those groups, and also higher than whites, on standardized tests.

Smart banks will position themselves to weather these stormy waters by reaching out to diverse markets.

They should also become more sophisticated about the legal and cultural challenges of running complex multi-ethnic organizations and serving complex multi-ethnic markets. For instance, is there risk in making loans to a small business that employs only members of the principal's own ethnic group? When—if ever—can lenders tailor credit standards and scorecards to particular ethnic groups in hopes of extending more credit to them? What do you do when an employee's traditional ethnic beliefs lead to reluctance to work for a supervisor from another nationality or religion, or for a woman? Should—and must—you permit employees to express their heritage in clothing outside your standard dress code, or to observe holidays that differ from the bank's?

Banks will confront these kinds of questions more often. They will also find that the answers to some, which had seemed to be matters of settled law and policy, are suddenly in doubt because of litigation or changing norms. Our increasingly multi-ethnic society will be a richer place, with more opportunity, but also one with a growing number of new risks and challenges.

Scholars Unearth New Field: White Studies[7]

By Laurent Belsie
Christian Science Monitor, August 14, 2001

When America confronts race, it casts a keen eye on blacks, Latinos, native Americans, Asians—everyone, it seems, except whites.

Whites have historically dominated the United States, and their ideas and values largely have shaped the culture. But only supremacists talk about "white culture." Everyone else keeps mum.

But in the past few years, some "white studies" scholars have begun breaking the silence. To understand the nation's racial diversity, they argue, it's crucial to understand the characteristics and privileges of America's largest racial group. Especially now, since for the first time white majority status looks threatened.

Hispanics—who are defined as an ethnicity, not a race, in the census—hold the key to the nation's demographic identity. If large numbers of them identify themselves as white, then white society will predominate in the U.S. (albeit with a Latino flavor) for decades to come. If Hispanics forge a separate identity, then somewhere around mid-century, the non-Hispanic white population will fall into minority status and the nation could enter a new era defined by a multicultural center.

"Whatever that racial center is, it's still going to be in many ways culturally white," says Jeff Hitchcock, executive director of the Center for the Study of White American Culture, a private nonprofit group based in Roselle, N.J. "But for someone who wants to be only white, it's going to be a little difficult for them."

Three out of 4 Americans describe themselves as exclusively white. Throw in the 5.5 million people who describe themselves as white as well as one or more other races, and the share climbs to 77.1 percent of the U.S. population—a higher proportion than existed in 1830.

Whites hold majorities in all but one state (Hawaii), according to a census report released Monday. Maine and Vermont have the largest white populations (97.9 percent). Mississippi (61.9 percent) and California (63.4 percent) have the smallest white majorities. Not

---

7. This article first appeared in *The Christian Science Monitor* on Aug. 14, 2001, and is reproduced with permission. Copyright © 2001 *The Christian Science Monitor*. All rights reserved. Online at *csmonitor.com*.

surprisingly, whites are concentrated in the 10 largest states, which happen to hold the most sway in electing American presidents. Of the 10 largest cities in the U.S., Phoenix has the highest proportion of whites (74 percent) followed by San Antonio (71 percent). Detroit has the lowest share (14 percent).

With such numerical advantage, it's little surprise that whites hold most of the levers of power in the U.S. But notions of white culture fell into disrepute with the civil rights movement of the 1960s. That's another reason few people talk of white culture nowadays—it sounds racist.

In fact, many minority scholars who study race welcome the emergence of white studies. "It's like putting a microscope on their culture," says Ray Winbush, director of the Race Relations Institute at historically black Fisk University in Nashville, Tenn. "We have black studies, women's studies, Latino studies. . . . The fact of

---

"It's like putting a microscope on their culture."—Ray Winbush, director of the Race Relations Institute at Fisk University

---

the matter is that white culture needs to be discussed in depth."

White studies experts face charges of being supremacists when, in fact, many of them espouse a move toward a multicultural society. (For example: Mr. Hitchcock, who is white, is married to a black sociologist, has two children of mixed race, and works for a minority-owned diversity consulting firm.) "You can talk about whiteness and white culture," he says. "And it's important to do so if we want to build a multiracial society."

Of course, the concept of whiteness changes over time. In 1790, the U.S. granted citizenship to "free white persons"—read: persons of Anglo-Saxon descent. Irish immigrants were discriminated against. Later, immigrants from Ireland, Italy, and elsewhere joined the establishment, to the exclusion of other minorities. Today, the census counts as white the original peoples of Europe, the Middle East, and North Africa. "Recognizing the historical fabrication, the changeability, and the contingencies of whiteness, we might begin to look in a new way upon race, the power relations it generates, and the social havoc it wreaks," writes Matthew Jacobson, a Yale University professor of American studies, in his 1998 book *Whiteness of a Different Color*.

The big question now looming is whether Latinos will expand even further the definition of whiteness. During the 19th century, census enumerators often lumped Hispanics with native Americans or "other." Only in the 1930 census, after a significant influx of Mexicans, did they gain their own category. Beginning with the 1940 census, however, Mexicans were listed as "white" unless they were definitely some other race.

This official inclusion of Hispanics as "white" continues today with two major differences. Since 1970, the job of determining race has been left up to the individuals themselves. Ever since 1980, the census has categorized Hispanics as an "ethnic" group—meaning people mark whether they're Hispanic in one question and then pick from 15 race categories in another. In the 2000 census, just over half of Hispanics identified themselves as white.

Many demographers expect Hispanics will be assimilated into white culture during the 21st century, just as southern Europeans were integrated during the 20th century. But white studies experts point to an intriguing counter-trend: whites' rising interest in ethnic distinctions, such as Irish-Americans and Italian-Americans.

According to this week's census report, white youths in particular show an increasing tendency to be identified as multiracial. For example: of the 5.5 million individuals who said they were white and at least one other race, 43 percent were under 18. By contrast, 24 percent of those who said they were white alone were under 18. "The question is: How far will it go?" Hitchcock says. "Will it take us to a multiracial society? I tend to be optimistic."

The New Seniors[8]

By Jay Rey
Buffalo News, September 10, 2001

If the mirror reveals more gray hair, your face shows more wrinkles and you move a bit slower, then you're in good company in the Buffalo Niagara region.

The exodus of thousands of young adults, who left behind their parents and grandparents, has made the Buffalo area what it is today: older.

Buffalo Niagara now has the 10th highest percentage of senior citizens among the nation's 103 metro areas with populations exceeding 500,000, census data shows. And the median age here is 38, three years older than in the rest of the nation.

"There are many older people who live alone and need help," said Josephine Asarese, 84, of the Town of Tonawanda, which has the area's highest percentage of seniors. "I have a lot of friends in the same situation. They don't want to give up their homes, but they probably should."

In fact, the 85-and-older bracket is the fastest growing segment of the region's population.

But don't let the numbers fool you, either. As more seniors live healthier and longer, many are bucking traditional stereotypes.

Bill O'Donnell, 73, of East Amherst, earned his black belt in tae kwon do this spring.

Richard Moot, 81, a longtime Buffalo attorney, has turned his attention to helping his peers enjoy their remaining years.

Eda Quigley of Kenmore taught herself to use a computer and continues to work part time for Erie County at the age of 90.

"I like to keep busy," Quigley said.

Still, a lot more than wrinkles and gray hair is at stake for this aging region.

Aside from national concerns, such as health care, prescription drugs and Social Security, Western New York's graying population faces a number of problems, including:

Housing: New senior citizen housing and retirement communities have boomed in recent years, but most monthly rents are beyond the blue-collar savings of much of the area's elderly population.

---

8. Article by Jay Rey from *Buffalo News* September 10, 2001. Copyright © *Buffalo News*.
Reprinted with permission.

Public services: Senior citizens eager to stay active are crowding community centers and recreation facilities—and stretching government budgets.

Growing isolation: Reaching out to elderly unable to leave their homes grows more difficult as more people live longer and more live alone.

Transportation: Getting a ride to the doctor's office and grocery store might be the biggest problem of all for local senior citizens.

"There's a couple different ways to look at it," said Mark Mather, a policy analyst with the Population Reference Bureau in Washington, D.C. "One is you need to do things to attract a younger generation to balance out the population more.

"The other," Mather said, "is you just have to refocus priorities so there's more focus on the older population."

Ageism is one of the obstacles Buffalo Niagara must hurdle in the years ahead, advocates say.

"There's a changing population and an absence of a plan," said Deputy Speaker Arthur O. Eve, 68. "There needs to be some serious, serious planning, from all levels of government, to deal with the needs of our growing senior population."

> *"There's a changing population and an absence of a plan."—* Arthur O. Eve, Deputy Speaker, New York State Assembly

Nation's older people

The nation's 65-and-older population increased in the past 10 years, but at a slower pace than in previous decades because of low birth rates during the late 1920s and early 1930s, demographers said.

Now, more than 12 percent of the U.S. population is older than 65. Here, the figure is 16 percent, compared with 8 percent a half-century ago.

"It's the fact that young people are leaving to take jobs elsewhere, getting an education and raising families elsewhere, leaving a region that's aging in place," Mather said.

While the area has fewer 60- to 64-year-olds—most likely snowbirds moving to warmer climates—many older Western New Yorkers favor the Buffalo area's familiar hometown confines over uprooting, experts said.

"I got a daughter in Arizona, a grandson in Vermont, one in Georgia," Asarese said. "But I was born in Buffalo, so I like it here. Everything is easy to reach. I know how to get around here. I don't know about someplace else."

The Town of Tonawanda and Cheektowaga each have a higher percentage of senior citizens than the Florida retirement haven of metropolitan St. Petersburg. Amherst's southeast corner and a pocket on its western edge have senior populations reaching 30 percent, census data shows.

Buffalo's population, meanwhile, is younger than that of its suburbs. The city lost more than 9,000 senior citizens in the 1990s because many moved to the suburbs or elsewhere, local experts said.

Dorothy Rogers has a son in Florida, but she prefers Kenmore.

"I've been to visit a few times," said Rogers, 85. "But it's too hot. I don't like the weather."

Housing for elderly

As a result, new housing for senior citizens and continuing-care facilities bloomed here the past decade. Many—at least in the suburbs—charge rents as high as $2,000 a month, which is far beyond what most seniors can afford, local experts said.

Communities also are noticing a decline in some of their housing stock, because the senior citizens who can't afford to rent an apartment don't have the money or ability to fix up their homes.

Amherst is trying to encourage more "affordable" senior housing, similar to the Hopkins Court Senior Living Community, where rents range from $479 to $568 a month plus utilities for a one- or two-bedroom apartment.

"I don't think you can build enough of this," said John E. "Skip" Cerio, Hopkins Court developer.

That's still too expensive, others said.

That's why Cayuga Village, subsidized housing in Cheektowaga with rents of $90 to $130 a month for low-income senior citizens, has a three-year waiting list.

"They can do more for themselves now because the stress of paying for high utilities and rent is off," said Midge Fournier, Cayuga's site manager.

Local governments face other pressures

Senior citizen tax breaks cost the Town of Tonawanda $137,000 this year, shifting the burden to the rest of the community. While that's not a huge loss, combine it with other town offerings—such as paramedic services or senior citizen programs—and the costs start adding up, officials said.

Town of Tonawanda senior citizens now can choose from 60 programs compared with about 40 a decade ago. Clarence is considering a new senior citizens center. Amherst built an $8 million senior citizens center last year.

"Seniors today look for more computer classes, art and music classes, language classes," said Mary Ellen Walsh, Amherst's senior citizen director. "It's a different group of people. They may have obtained a higher level of education, so their interests are different."

Reaching the frail

As the local population ages, reaching the frail elderly becomes tougher.

> *As the local population ages, reaching the frail elderly becomes tougher.*

Seven percent of the region's 65 and over population lives in nursing homes or other group quarters, but nearly 32 percent lives alone, census numbers show.

"What we're finding is more elderly who are living alone because a lot of children are out of the area," said Bonnie McMorrow, director of social work of Meals on Wheels of Buffalo and Erie County.

While the outreach program provides 1,800 elderly with two meals a day, it still has a waiting list.

"You have a lot of people living alone who have dementia, but because of the nature of the disease they don't think they need help," said Nancy Schenk, who coordinates Amherst's senior outreach program. "So things like paying bills, housekeeping and driving become problems for them."

Transportation may be the biggest problem

While Erie County and its localities provide a patchwork van service for a small fee, the service is in such demand it often meets only the most urgent needs, such as doctor appointments.

Patricia Wojcik, Cheektowaga's senior citizen director, recently sought outside help, asking a local supermarket chain to offer seniors transportation to its store.

"There's a lot being done for seniors, but it's not adequate for the need," Schenk said.

Oldest group grows fastest

Amid the region's changing population has emerged a more diverse group of senior citizens.

As people live longer, the span between the "younger" seniors and the 85-and-older group—the fastest growing segment of the population—has increased.

Buffalo Niagara's over-85 population grew 34 percent in the past 10 years, mirroring a national trend.

Medical advances and improved diet and exercise help people live longer, experts said.

"I had some time on my hands, so I decided to tone up," Peter Giallombardo, 69, a retired optician from Williamsville, said as he left the Town of Tonawanda Aquatic and Fitness Center one day recently. "I come here at least four times a week to swim or do some light weightlifting."

Erie County even embarked on a senior citizens fitness program last year. Coordinator Richard Derwald—a 66-year-old personal trainer—stresses the importance of stretching to increase flexibility and to avoid falls that often lead to more serious health complications.

"People are more conscious of taking care of their body—walking, exercising, riding bikes. They read and hear on T.V. that exercise will help you live longer so they just automatically do it," said Ray Pfeiffer, 78, who works part time for the Town of Tonawanda senior citizens center.

"When my father retired, he never exercised. He just vegetated," Pfeiffer recalled.

One of the biggest problems for the Buffalo area may be fighting ageism, said Pamela Krawczyk, Erie County's director of senior services.

Too often an aging community is viewed negatively, but Buffalo Niagara and its employers could afford to tap into its older generation, she said.

O'Donnell, Quigley and Moot provide proof.

"There's a great resource out there," Krawczyk said. "We have to lose the view that the gray hair means the rocking chair, nursing homes and bingo."

Wave of School-Age Children to Flood Nation's Classrooms[9]

By Genaro C. Armas
Houston Chronicle, May 23, 2001

More than 20 million children will reach high school age in four years, posing daunting challenges for school districts already coping with classroom crowding and teacher shortages.

Nationally, the number of children age 10 to 14 increased 20 percent in the past decade, to 20.5 million, according to the 2000 census. A 10-year-old in 2000 would be 14 in 2004, the age by which most students start high school.

The number of children age 4 and under—those who will be able to start elementary school over the next four years—increased 4 percent to 19.2 million in 2000.

"We are finding even more schools in more places holding classes in hallways, and increasing class sizes in an age when we are talking about the need to reduce it," said Kathleen Lyons, spokeswoman for the National Education Association.

Preparing for the expected onslaught of students "really comes down to finances," she said.

The 10-to-14 category—children of the large baby boom generation—increased in nearly all states. The nation's fastest-growing states saw surges in the under-5 population as well, as booming economies drew young couples from other states.

And both age brackets were affected by a higher-than-projected count of Hispanics, much of it due to immigration, analysts said.

Nevada had an 83 percent increase in children age 10 to 14 during the decade, and a 58 percent rise in the number of kids age 4 and under.

Arizona's 10-to-14 population grew 46 percent, while its 4-and-under population increased 31 percent during the same span.

Jennifer Schmidt, the mother of a high school sophomore and a 1-year-old, said things have to improve soon no matter what the reason for the increase.

"I just found out my daughter doesn't have a place to sit during lunchtime—she sits in the hallway," said Schmidt, of Silver Spring, Md. The 10-to-14 population in this Washington suburb increased 33 percent during the 1990s.

---

9. Reprinted with permission of *The Associated Press*.

"When my 1-year-old gets to that age, we've been thinking about moving or putting him through private school," she said.

Crowding, teacher shortages and inadequate instruction for non-English-speaking students are challenges schools in New York, Chicago and Los Angeles have long encountered. Now those issues are causing headaches in 1990s boom areas like Las Vegas.

The Clark County, Nev., school district, which includes Las Vegas, forecasts it will add between 10,000 and 15,000 new students a year. Ten new school buildings opened this school year, with 15 new ones scheduled to be completed by the end of next school year.

Cartwright Elementary School in Las Vegas had 21 portable classrooms in its playground last school year to help educate 1,400 students—over 700 more than capacity.

Schools that opened nearby helped ease the burden this school year, reducing Cartwright's enrollment to 880, requiring just six portable classrooms.

"It's been very challenging. We try to do as little disruption as possible for the kids," said Cartwright's principal, Emily Aguero. "But when you come and look at the growth out here, parents know that there isn't really much choice."

Lyons said the federal government can lift part of the burden by stepping in to build new schools. Other solutions that have long been proposed include better pay and benefits to hire and retain new teachers.

Demographers have attributed much of the population growth in children to a higher-than-expected count of Hispanics in most states. The number of Hispanics under age 18 increased 59 percent during the decade, with North Carolina's 401 percent gain larger than any other state.

"Many of those unexpected children were Hispanic. They are the children of those families who immigrated" to the United States during the 1990s, said demographer Martha Farnsworth Riche, a former head of the Census Bureau.

Men Make a Numerical Comeback[10]

By Laurent Belsie
Christian Science Monitor, June 20, 2001

After seeing their share of the population fall for more than a century, men are staging a comeback in the United States.

From a historical low in 1980, the ratio of men to women is moving slowly back up. New census data show that last year the nation boasted 96.3 men per 100 women—up from 94.5 in 1980. The swing is unusual for a country with a maturing population—and a sharp contrast with other developed and developing countries.

This re-balancing represents a sign of demographic health, population experts say, because it means the U.S. does not face imminent danger from either extreme in the gender balance.

In Europe, by contrast, an aging population, dominated by women, threatens to bankrupt social and pension programs, as fewer workers support more retirees. In South Asia, some observers worry that a young, male-heavy population could one day grow restless, sparking unrest or even war.

But America's male resurgence remains uneven. Non-Latino males continue to see their share of the population fall. Minority males, particularly Hispanic men, have sparked the turnaround.

The move comes as something of a surprise. "As the baby boom [moves] up the age ladder, you'd actually expect the reverse," says Carl Haub, a demographer at the Population Reference Bureau in Washington.

Factors behind the change

That's because, typically, women live longer than men, so aging societies become feminized. By contrast, countries with very young populations tend to be male-dominated because more boys are born than girls. On average, about 105 males are born for every 100 females.

But America's unexpected rise in immigration—plus a better count of minority men in the 2000 census—probably accounts for most of the change, he adds.

---

10. This article first appeared in *The Christian Science Monitor* on June 20, 2001, and is reproduced with permission. Copyright © 2001 *The Christian Science Monitor*. All rights reserved. Online at *csmonitor.com*.

Demographers remain guarded, because the data are still dribbling out of the U.S. Census Bureau. Today, the bureau released detailed numbers on eight more states plus the District of Columbia, bringing the released total to 10 states. National figures will be released later this summer. With one-fifth of the states reporting, the trends seem clear.

Take Illinois. The share of males among non-Hispanic whites stood at 94.9 last year. But a nearly 70 percent surge in the state's Hispanic population during the 1990s is rebalancing that ratio. Latino men outnumber Latino women 112.3 to 100 in the state. That allowed the state's overall male-female ratio to climb from 94.5 in 1990 to 95.9 last year.

Males also predominate in Hispanic populations in Indiana, Louisiana, Montana, Nebraska, and Nevada. Even in states where

---

The Census Bureau also appears to have done a much better job of counting minority males compared with the 1990 count.

Latino women hold the edge, the gap is smaller than among non-Latino whites. That means a rise in Latino populations pushes the male-to-female ratio upward.

The Census Bureau also appears to have done a much better job of counting minority males compared with the 1990 count. Even using a stricter definition for 2000 than in 1990, the African-American population in Illinois climbed 10.8 percent.

It's not clear whether the trend will create more male-dominant states.

In 1990, only Alaska, California, Hawaii, Nevada, and Wyoming had more men than women. Data haven't been released yet for four of the five. In Nevada, where 2000 data have been released, the male share edged up a bit from 103.7 in 1990—then the second-highest ratio in the country—to 103.9. Alaska had the highest ratio of males in 1990, with 111.4 men per 100 women. Mississippi had the lowest ratio: 91.7 males per 100.

One of the likeliest candidates to join the male-dominant club—Montana—has moved within a whisker of achieving a 50-50 split between the sexes.

Although the male-female ratio is more balanced in a few less-developed countries, such as Cuba and Thailand, the U.S. situation remains fairly balanced compared with other areas of the world.

During most of its own history—as a young, developing nation—the U.S. boasted more men than women. One factor, in addition to the higher number of boy babies than girls, was the large number of women who died in childbirth.

America's 1950 shift

But in 1950, as the nation matured, the pendulum moved the other direction and women predominated. Demographers argue that the swing has much more to do with the greater longevity of women than, say, the ravages of World War II or Vietnam. By 1980, the ratio reached its nadir of 94.5 males per 100 females. By moving back up to 96.3 per 100 last year, the nation is showing a healthy resilience against trends that are besetting other developed countries.

Russia, for example, counts only 88.1 men for every 100 women. The situation remains a little unusual because that nation lost so many men during World War II. But the real challenge is that Russia's elderly population is growing while its number of babies is falling precipitously.

Italy retains a respectable male-female ratio—94.4 per 100—but it, too, faces rapid aging and a baby bust. That will likely boost the share of women. More important, it portends financial trouble, as fewer workers try to support a growing number of retirees drawing pensions and health benefits.

Italy "is basically preprogrammed for decline," says Mr. Haub of the Population Reference Bureau.

If Europe's future includes a rising proportion of elderly women, South Asia faces exactly the opposite problem: a surplus of young men. The young populations and cultural preferences for male children have produced a marked imbalance in India and South Korea. China's one-baby-per-family program has exacerbated the problem in the world's most populous country. As a result, China's latest census counted 106.7 males for every 100 females.

"Already in China, they have an increasing problem of women being kidnapped," says Jim Vittitow of the Population Research Institute, a nonprofit organization in Front Royal, Va. "You also will have, as time goes on, a huge number of men who are frustrated. . . . And that will be a cauldron that will eventually boil over. It could cause massive unrest or be directed outward."

If the U.S. is heading back to equilibrium, then such problems look less likely, researchers suggest.

Still, they caution that it's too early to conclude that there will be a full male rebound. "We've seen it since '80," says Renee Spraggins, a statistician with the Census Bureau. "It may be taking that turn."

III. Where We Live Now

Figure 8

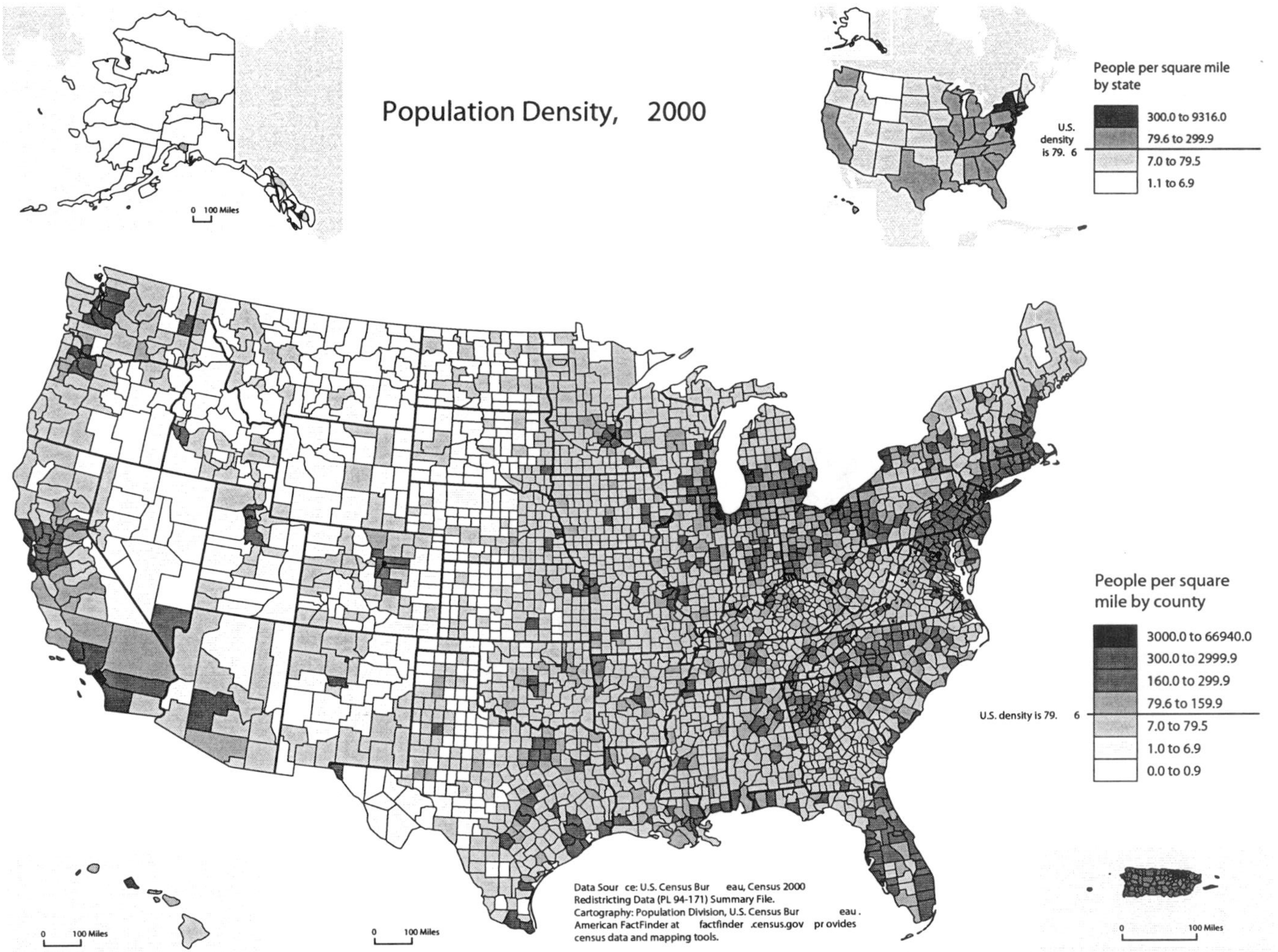
Population Density, 2000
0 100 Miles
People per square mile by state
U.S. density is 79.6
300.0 to 9316.0
79.6 to 299.9
7.0 to 79.5
1.1 to 6.9
People per square mile by county
U.S. density is 79.6
3000.0 to 66940.0
300.0 to 2999.9
160.0 to 299.9
79.6 to 159.9
7.0 to 79.5
1.0 to 6.9
0.0 to 0.9
0 100 Miles
0 100 Miles
0 100 Miles
Data Sour ce: U.S. Census Bur eau, Census 2000 Redistricting Data (PL 94-171) Summary File.
Cartography: Population Division, U.S. Census Bur eau.
American FactFinder at factfinder .census.gov pr ovides census data and mapping tools.

Editor's Introduction

I f all the people in the United States—men, women, and children—were scattered evenly across the land, each person would stand in the midst of approximately eight square acres. Of course, this is not the case. People like to live in groups. They cluster in villages and towns and crowd into big cities. They also move from one part of the country to another, searching for work, for a more comfortable life, or for a community where they can feel at home.

The 2000 census confirmed a process that had already been observed in earlier counts: a gradual shift of population from the relatively crowded Northeast and Midwest toward the "Sunbelt"—the states of the South, Southwest, and Far West. Demographers generally agree that this shift reflects the loss of manufacturing jobs in older industries, which are located mainly in what is now called "the Rustbelt." But jobs are not the only factor in this migration. Many retirees in the North would like to hang up their snow shovels for good, and people of all ages may dream of a more casual lifestyle in a less densely developed landscape.

The 2000 census introduced an interesting variation on this migration pattern, in that the states which made the most dramatic gains in population—Nevada, Arizona, Idaho, Utah, Colorado, and Georgia—were not central to the original Sunbelt at all but well out on its fringes. In his article "Shifts in Political Power," demographer William Frey dubs these states the "New Sunbelt" and describes their appeal to domestic migrants (mostly white)—an appeal comparable to the lure of the suburbs after World War II. Frey also notes that diversity is tied to geography all across the country, since immigrants tend to remain close to their fellow nationals in burgeoning multi-ethnic "gateway" areas (at least until someone they know has established a foothold somewhere else), while areas of slow growth show little if any change in ethnic profile. These conditions, he says, are leading toward an America of new regional differences and new political constituencies. In "With an Asian Influx, a Suburb Finds Itself Transformed," Patricia Leigh Brown visits one of Frey's "melting pots," a Los Angeles satellite city that attracts Asian immigrants from around the globe. Mark Dolliver suggests that the "Edward Scissorhands" stereotype of the suburbs may be out of date in "Guess Where You'll Find the Melting Pot Today?" In "African-Americans Turn and Head South," James T. Mulder describes another significant migratory trend, the return of African Americans to a changed South, and Glen Martin surveys the Dakota Territory today in "Where the Buffalo Roam, Again." As the last article makes clear, this is a part of the United States where population is actually thinning out (to the benefit of wildlife); only the Native American sector of the population shows a healthy rate of growth. Significantly, the animals that Native Americans once prized are beginning to be cultivated as a key element for the region's economic future.

Shifts in Political Power[1]

By WILLIAM H. FREY
WORLD & I, MAY 2001

The numbers released from the 2000 census, along with the results of last November's presidential election, are shaping a new regional paradigm for understanding the nation's political landscape. At the center of this change is the rise of the "New Sunbelt" as a distinct demographic and political force.

In the past, the conventional wisdom of political geography pitted largely Democratic, liberal-leaning cities against their primarily Republican, conservative-trending suburbs. For decades, big-city-backed mayors and legislative representatives espoused issues that catered to their minority, blue-collar, and labor-union constituencies, while suburban politicians favored the causes of their mostly white, middle-class populations, such as less federal interference, lower taxes, and greater local autonomy.

To be sure, there were regional overlays to this divide. The conservative Democratic solid South gave way to the conservative Republican solid South, holding regionally distinct economic and social perspectives throughout. As well, northeasterners held more distinctly liberal regional points of view that differed sharply from the predilections and voting patterns of their counterparts in the right-leaning South, more independent West, and middle-of-the-road heartland states.

Yet within each region, the division between city and suburb formed a bright boundary line. A suburban residence represented the symbol of success for generations of families that aspired to a middle-class lifestyle that they could share with neighbors who shared like values. This stood in contrast to the demographically heterogeneous city population, comprising the very poor and very rich, minorities and immigrants, young professional singles and older retirees—all lacking the desire or wherewithal to relocate to the more comfortable suburbs.

The new census and recent election results suggest the emergence of a regional equivalent of the suburbs. That is, there is a migration of largely middle-class white and African-American households away from the old, congested, expensive suburbs of the Northeast and West Coast regions toward low-density communities of all sizes in the nation's southeastern and less urbanized western states. Like

---

1. Article by William H. Frey from *World & I* May 2001. Copyright © *World & I*. Reprinted with permission.

the early suburbanites, these new interregional movers are still in quest of an easier lifestyle and co-residence with citizens who share their basic values and more middle-class political views.

At first glance, this migration might be thought of as an extension of the long-term redistribution of population from the Frostbelt (Northeast and Midwest regions) to the Sunbelt (South and West regions). But upon closer inspection of the new census results, recent migration statistics, and the November 2000 election outcomes, it appears that these movers are creating a new suburban-like category of states that can be termed the "New Sunbelt."

These states lie at the periphery of the historically prominent Sunbelt destination states: California, Texas, and Florida. While these three states still attract migrants, they have become much more urbanized; the source of their growth has increasingly been dominated by immigration from abroad rather than from other parts of the United States. This is especially the case for California, which

---

New Sunbelt states are characterized by growth via migration from other parts of the United States.

---

has recently lost more domestic migrants than it gained.

New Sunbelt states are characterized by growth via migration from other parts of the United States. It has risen sharply in the past decade and comprises middle-class, younger, and well-off baby-boom households that hold middle-of-the-road views on social and economic issues. This exodus from suburbs of more cosmopolitan, liberal-leaning urban areas on the coasts will forge increasing divides—demographic, cultural, and political—between the states of the New Sunbelt and the more congested "melting-pot states" located in the old Sunbelt and Northeast.

The 2000 census results point up the ascendancy of these New Sunbelt states in terms of their population growth and political clout. The fastest-growing states of the 1990s were Nevada, Arizona, Colorado, Utah, Idaho, and Georgia; each increased its growth significantly over the 1980s. North Carolina, another rapidly rising New Sunbelt state, increased its growth from 12 percent in the 1980s to 22 percent in the 1990s. Each of the New Sunbelt states increased its population growth substantially in the past decade.

The reapportionment of Congress, with the new census, points up the increased political importance of the New Sunbelt states. Seven of the 12 congressional seats that shifted between states went to the New Sunbelt: Arizona, 2 seats; Georgia, 2 seats; and Nevada, Colorado, and North Carolina, 1 seat each. The remaining 5 seats went to the premier old Sunbelt states: Texas, Florida, and California. (This is down from a collective gain of 14 seats for these three states after the 1990 census-based reapportionment.)

Moreover, the results of the recent presidential election showed that all but three (Washington, Oregon, Delaware) of the New Sunbelt states favored the Republican candidate, George W. Bush. Democratic candidate Al Gore won both the most populous "melting-pot" states (California, New York, New Jersey, New Mexico, and Hawaii) and those in the slow-growing parts of the country (Illinois, Pennsylvania, Michigan, Massachusetts, Connecticut, Wisconsin, Minnesota, Iowa, Maine, and Vermont).

The discussion below will describe recent population-movement patterns that are contributing to the new political geography. It suggests that different constituencies will emerge in regions we class as the New Sunbelt, melting-pot states, and slow-growing states that are located largely in the Snowbelt.

Different constituencies will emerge in regions we class as the New Sunbelt, melting-pot states, and slow-growing states.

The results are based on a new analysis of state and regional shifts in the voting-age population for the period between the 1990 census and November 7, 2000 (Election Day). They also draw from analysis of migration and distribution patterns for states and demographic groups based on the U.S. Census Bureau's Current Population Survey for the years 1990–99.

White shifts to the New Sunbelt

Since 1990, the white voting-age population increased by more than 22 percent in Nevada, Utah, Idaho, Arizona, and Colorado. Thirty-six percent of the nation's gain in the white voting-age population took place in the non-California West. Georgia, the Carolinas, and Tennessee increased their white voting-age populations by more than twice the national rate (5.5 percent).

The flows of voters to these "New West" and "New South" states arrive from all parts of the country, but the dominant origins are California and metropolitan New York. (From 1990 to 1999, California contributed to 71 percent of net white migration gains to the "rest of the West"; New York and New Jersey contributed to 65 percent of net white migration gains for southeastern states.) They infuse new destinations with "suburban" demographic attributes that should reinforce middle-class, moderately conservative voting constituencies that already exist in those areas.

The West is also noted for its attraction of young itinerant profes-sionals who are "lone eagles" and thus tend to be more independent-minded about politics. A third group of new arrivals to both the West and Southeast are white retirees with some resources. While probably economically conservative, they like to be assured of the solvency of the Social Security system.

The white arrivees to both these New Sunbelt regions may share some suburban, middle-of-the-road values with the "homegrown" whites, but their more cosmopolitan origins may make them more socially liberal and less supportive of such issues as gun control (in the West) or abortion (in the South). In the latter region, the influx of new suburban whites is accompanied by another new influx that should moderate the social tenor of political discourse: the return migration of northern blacks.

Blacks return to the South

Blacks are also moving to the New Sunbelt but predominantly to the South. The 1990s represented something of a full-circle shift with respect to black migration, countering a trend that character-ized most of the last century. Blacks from all other census regions (Northeast, Midwest, and West) descended into the South in greater numbers than those who left. Between 1990 and 1999, the South received a net gain in black voting-age migrants of 326,225 from the rest of the United States.

On Election Day 2000, 53 percent of the nation's black voting-age population resided in the South. This movement is made up of mid-dle-class blacks drawn to the booming New South economies, work-ing-class blacks who were let go because of manufacturing restructuring in the North, and black retirees who were more com-fortable relocating in southern communities than in western ones.

Yet, it is the increasing numbers of baby-boomer professional blacks who will help draw the tone of both Republican and Demo-cratic appeals toward middle-of-the-road economic issues and away from the more strident, thinly disguised racial politics of the past. While African-American newcomers will certainly be receptive to traditional black Democratic constituency issues like affirmative action, the middle-class, suburban segments of these newcomers will also be receptive to more moderate proposals like targeted tax cuts, school vouchers, and partial privatization of Social Security. By the same token, the new white migrants will be less likely to side with longtime residents on culturally conservative issues.

The reconsolidation of blacks in the South, along with the new in-migration of northern suburban whites, will make the South a dis-tinct but more progressive region than in the past. The southern states we have classed as part of the New Sunbelt are emblematic of these new trends. On Election Day 2000, their voting-age population was 22 percent black, 74 percent white, and less than 4 percent Hispanic and Asian.

Melting-pot states

Surely, a dramatic migration-related change in the nation's electorate since 1990 is the infusion of new immigrant minorities. Between the 1990 census and Election

> *More significant is the concentration of this growth [in immigrants] in only a few states.*

Day 2000, the combined voting-age populations of Hispanics and Asians increased by 9.6 million to 29.5 million overall.

More significant is the concentration of this growth in only a few states. California, Texas, Florida, and New York garnered 61 percent of these gains and now house almost two-thirds of the combined Hispanic and Asian population. These states, combined with New Jersey, Hawaii, and New Mexico, are identified as melting-pot states and represent a very different constituency than those in other parts of the country. Non-Hispanic whites make up only 61 percent of potential voters, while Hispanics and Asians constitute 29 percent of the voting-age population in these states.

It is true that new immigrant minorities tend to vote in significantly lower numbers than the remaining population. Nonetheless, both Bush and Gore paid attention to these changing demographics when visiting each of these melting-pot states—symbolically, by speaking Spanish when visiting Hispanic neighborhoods, and in their policy prescriptions, favoring INS reform, improved public education, and support for family values.

Both were aware of California's dramatic Republican-to-Democratic shift in state offices, which was due, in part, to perceived anti-immigration sentiment attributed to Republican Gov. Pete Wilson. And the Hispanic and Asian share of the Golden State's voting-age population is projected to increase from 40 percent in November 2000 to 52 percent in 2015.

Immigration is not the only cause for the rise of Hispanic and Asian visibility in the melting-pot states. New York, New Jersey, and California exhibited a decline and out-migration of their white voting-age populations over the course of the 1990s. This reflects, in large measure, the exodus to the New Sunbelt and helps to cement demographic differences in the constituencies of both groups of states.

Slow-growing states

Much attention has been given to the dominant destination states for immigrants, white suburbanites, and African Americans. Still, there is a broad swath of states in the interior part of the country whose gains in voting-age populations have been relatively modest. The voting-age population of each of these states has grown slower than the national rate (11.4 percent) between the 1990 census and Election Day 2000.

The importance of these slow-growing and declining states for the recent election and those in the future cannot be diminished. One reason is that they are strategic states. Despite Bush's victories in Texas and Florida, most melting-pot states are likely to tilt toward more liberal issues that tend to be associated with Democrats.

> *The states that will be most up for grabs are part of this "slow-growing" group.*

Similarly, the changing demographics of the New Sunbelt states are likely to keep them in the columns of more moderate and conservative Republican candidates. The states that will be most up for grabs are part of this "slow-growing" group.

Further, key demographic segments that were recently designated as important "swing-voter" groups have an accentuated presence within these states. This is because the demography of slow-growing states exaggerates the importance of groups that have not moved out to faster-growing parts of the country. Thus, modestly growing states have larger shares of older, more middle income, and whiter populations than other parts of the country.

Three swing-voter groups with a large presence in these states are white working wives, white "forgotten majority" men and white seniors. The first two groups have long been taken for granted by Democrats and Republicans. According to political analysts Ruy Teixeira and Joel Rogers, authors of *America's Forgotten Majority: Why the White Working Class Still Matters* (Basic Books, 2000), these groups seem to have gotten lost in the shuffle as more attention was paid to upscale "soccer moms" in the 1992 and '96 presidential races.

Both major presidential contenders courted these groups by emphasizing "compassionate" policies or a willingness to fight for working-class families. The third group, white seniors, tends to vote in high percentages. Their vote was also courted by both candidates, who wished to assure them that Social Security would remain solvent and that they would not have to absorb high prices for prescription drugs.

From a demographic perspective, the significance of all three groups is inflated because they reside in key "battleground" states from which disproportionate numbers of younger, minority, or more upscale groups have moved away. This can be seen by looking at the share of each of these three groups in the combined voting populations of six "battleground" states (Pennsylvania, Ohio, Michigan, Illinois, Wisconsin, and Missouri).

Together, the three groups represented 53 percent of the voting-age population of these states. In contrast, they constitute only 36 percent of the voting-age population of melting-pot states and only 46 percent of the total U.S. voting-age population. It is small wonder that both presidential candidates paid so much attention to these demographic groups.

The new regional politics

Recent migration and immigration patterns are shaping new demographic divides across the country. The directed destinations of middle-class and upscale white suburbanites to the New Sunbelt, the migration of blacks to the South, the clustering of new ethnic minorities in melting-pot states, and an expanded number of slow-growth states with increasingly older, whiter populations are creating sharp regional divides with distinct sets of constituencies and issues. More so than in the past, presidential candidates' speeches, public-service announcements, and debates are seen nationwide and thus play quite differently in various areas.

No wonder the candidates for the presidency were careful in crafting their messages so as to appeal to but not offend important groups within these different regions. Who would not agree with a candidate espousing to be "a uniter and not a divider"? Or one who is not afraid to display traditional family values via frequent public displays of affection with his spouse? In the politics of the future, with the regions becoming more demographically distinct, national presidential campaigns will become ever more careful balancing acts.

With an Asian Influx, a Suburb Finds Itself Transformed[2]

BY PATRICIA LEIGH BROWN
NEW YORK TIMES, MAY 26, 2001

It is hard to pin down the elusive tipping point when the old Fremont gave way to the new one.

Maybe it was when Hillside Drive was renamed Gurdwara Road, for the Gurdwara Sahib Temple, which Sikh residents built there. Mayor Gus Morrison recalled the discussion: "At a public meeting, someone got up and said, 'I can't pronounce Gurdwara.' Then a Sikh stands up and says, 'I can't pronounce Paseo Padre,'" referring to a major thoroughfare.

Or perhaps it was during the spate of burglaries of upper-end Asian homes when the city, on the advice of a Chinese-American citizens' group, placed advertisements in local Asian newspapers suggesting that families leave shoes on the porch when going out.

"We finally figured out the crooks knew if they didn't see shoes on the front porch, no one was home," said Chief Craig Steckler of the Police Department.

Whenever it was, there is little doubt that over the last 10 years, a blue-collar, lily-white, somewhat anonymous bedroom community, once best known for churning out Chevys and Toyotas, has essentially disappeared. In its place has arisen something dazzlingly different: a magnet for immigrants.

The city is a vivid example of a shift in the landscape as Asian immigrants, particularly new arrivals with professional degrees and entrepreneurial ambitions, forsake urban enclaves and move to the suburbs in such numbers that they transform them.

The new Fremonters include Silicon Valley engineers, entrepreneurs of every persuasion—from Sikhs owning 7-Eleven stores to Chinese chief executives living in Mediterranean palazzos—as well as Fijian Indians, Filipinos and one of the country's largest concentrations of Afghan refugees. The latest census figures disclose that the Asian population doubled since 1990 in this city of 206,000 people, to 37 percent from 19 percent.

---

2. Article by Patricia Leigh Brown from *New York Times* May 26, 2001. Copyright © *New York Times*. Reprinted with permission.

And as change has come to Fremont, where orchards and cauliflower fields have been replaced by boulevards and 5,000-square-foot homes, an intense learning curve has followed, one likely to be replicated in many corners of America.

Nationally, the percentage of growth of the Asian population was 58 percent from 1990 to 2000, and Asians now account for 4 percent of the population. Among cities of more than 100,000 people, Fremont is one of five with the highest percentage of Asian residents.

The city, incorporated in 1956 from five towns, is trying to adapt to the multitude of cultures in its midst, people with widely differing circumstances, customs and worldviews.

At the elite Mission San Jose High School, whose students are 61 percent Asian, and where the senior class has 17 students tied for valedictorian, signs for the school election—"Amanda Chan for Class Treasurer," "Sadaf Gowani for Secretary"—reflect the transformed city.

As change has come to Fremont, . . . an intense learning curve has followed.

So did last summer's Fourth of July parade, when a Sikh float decorated with a model of the Golden Temple in India took its place alongside those of the Furry Friends animal rescue group and the All Stars Cheerleading Squad.

But it has not gone off without a hitch. Two years ago, three white teenagers sprayed swastikas and white-pride slogans on a synagogue and a high school. Last year, county school officials rejected a move by some parents in the affluent Mission Peak neighborhood to create their own school district, which would have been over 60 percent Asian, partly because it would have created "an enclave of privilege."

Like much of the Bay Area, Fremont, where the mean household income has risen to $93,000 from $71,000 a decade ago, is short on moderately priced housing. The average rent for a one-bedroom apartment is $1,400. This has profoundly affected Fremont's 20,000 Afghan refugees, among them an increasing number of professional women who have fled the country's ruling Taliban and relocated here through a United Nations program.

In one of many new rituals here, Afghan women meet at a community center on Wednesdays, after exercise class in their high heels and chador, or head-to-toe cloaks, and support one another over chapli kebab and coffee cake.

The city's newness and lack of physical cohesiveness—there is no downtown—may have served it well.

"There weren't that many old places to undo, and there's been a dedication to fitting everybody in," said John Landis, a professor of city and regional planning at the University of California. "Fremont is not afraid of growth and not afraid of change. That makes it unusual in California."

The complex dance of cultures has changed here in hundreds of tiny ways. On a typical morning, Sikhs recite the morning prayers, or nitnem, on a live radio broadcast from the temple, while a few miles away, Thai Buddhist monks in saffron robes chant in another new temple.

But tensions percolate amid resplendent architecture. Every year, at the "Festival of India," which has become a mainstream event in the city, Sikhs demonstrate for Khalistan, an independent nation they hope to carve out of India's Punjab State.

Another highly emotional issue flared up in Fremont schools over kirpans, the sacred ceremonial swords signifying baptism, which are worn by Sikhs from childhood on. When some parents challenged a school district policy permitting the wearing of kirpans under certain conditions, Sikhs and the Fremont police worked out an agreement. Now they can be worn on a chain if concealed beneath an outer garment and wired into a scabbard. The blade must be blunted and be no longer than three and a half inches.

"It's a compromise we're doing for now," said Jagmeet Kaur, who is active in the Sikh community. "But it's not acceptable, really."

Chief Steckler finds himself embroiled in issues he never imagined.

Three years ago, the department broke up a melee in a parking lot after representatives of the Taliban spoke at a local mosque.

The police have also worked with the local Afghan Coalition and Afghan Women's Association to educate newcomers on child abuse, spousal abuse and other family and social issues.

Corporal punishment of children, widely accepted in Afghanistan, "can be a violation of law in California," Chief Steckler said. The city has sponsored community meetings about where corporal punishment ends and child abuse begins.

Many old-time Fremonters speak of how their lives have been broadened by the town's transformation. Yet some find it bewildering.

"You get to learn a lot about different nations," said Lindsey Johnson, a freshman at Mission San Jose High School. "But then it gets frustrating when you're in the minority. My best friend and I are blonde, light-eyed and in honors' classes.

"When we walk into the room you can tell from the body language they're thinking, 'Why are you in this class?'"

John Sullivan, who was recently laid off from his job at a biomedical company, reflected on his city of 40 years, saying:

"A lot has been gained. But when jobs are displaced and people see immigrants living in the hills and young people leaving because they can't afford to live here, it has to cause resentment. It's human nature."

Fremont, where more than 1,200 new high-tech businesses flourished over the past decade, has been buffeted by the recent economic downturns. Some start-ups have shut down; others have laid off workers. The layoffs are affecting skilled engineers and programmers from India and elsewhere who flocked here on work visas, an unknown number of whom are leaving the Bay Area or returning home.

Politics have yet to mirror the changed city. The five-member City Council has one Chinese-American.

"Very rarely do immigrant populations get integrated into the political system," said Richard Orsi, a history professor at California State University in nearby Hayward. "In Fremont, many of them are accomplished professionals leading busy lives. But it will come."

Jagmeet Kaur has lived in England and Canada but says she feels most at home in Fremont. "I see history," she said, standing outside the Gurdwara Sahib Temple. "I see my culture. It's all here."

Guess Where You'll Find the Melting Pot Today?[3]

By Mark Dolliver
ADWEEK EASTERN EDITION, JULY 16, 2001

It's probably too much to hope that mere facts can undo the stereo-type of suburbia as a redoubt of white-bread white folks. Neverthe-less, this image has been overtaken by events. Analyzing data from the 2000 census, a report by the Brookings Institution Center on Urban & Metropolitan Policy makes clear how heterogeneous the suburbs have become. Minority groups last year accounted for 27.3 percent of the suburban population in the 102 largest metropolitan areas; 47 percent of minority-group residents in those metros lived in the suburbs. In fact, says the report, "Minorities were responsible for the bulk of suburban population gains in a majority of the metro areas studied." In the 102 metros, blacks last year constituted 8.4 percent of all suburbanites, Hispanics 12.1 percent and Asians 4.4 percent. Putting the matter another way, 38.8 percent of black resi-dents in these metros lived in the burbs, as did 49.6 percent of His-panics and 54.6 percent of Asians. Meanwhile, some major-metro suburbs lost white population during the 1990s. In several of these—including Miami, San Francisco and Los Angeles-Long Beach—"the rate of white loss in the suburbs exceeded that in the central cities." Marketers and other purveyors of pop culture give little sign of having noticed all these changes. (One suspects, for instance, that those who use "urban" as a synonym for "black" can't do the best job of connecting with nonwhites who live in the burbs.) Why has the image of suburbia lagged so far behind demographic reality? In part, there's a natural time lag in the minds of those city slickers who produce most pop culture. The last time they spent much time in a suburb was when they were kids—i.e., a decade or two or three ago. But there's more going on than that. Too many urbanites have invested too much psychic energy in feeling superior to suburbia. For them, it must remain a nightmarish enclave of homogeneity—a Hartsdale of Darkness. The real suburbia of today is too complicated to satisfy this simple need.

---

3. Article by Mark Dolliver from *Adweek* July 16, 2001. Copyright © *Adweek*. Reprinted with permission.

African-Americans Turn and Head South

Retirees and College Graduates Are Finding Opportunities in a New South[4]

By James T. Mulder
The Post-Standard, March 16, 2000

Johnny Denham left Mississippi in 1955 and headed north to find a decent job and escape racial prejudice.

He lived briefly in Michigan and Wisconsin before moving to Syracuse in 1960. He got a job here as a mechanic at East Syracuse Chevrolet, where he worked for 33 years.

After retiring, Denham returned to the South. In 1996, he moved back to his hometown of Hickory, Miss., a rural community with a population of 493 people. The 63-year-old spends his days there cultivating his garden, hunting and fishing. "I really enjoy it down here," he said.

Denham is part of a dramatic turnaround in national African-American migration trends. More blacks are moving South these days, reversing the massive African-American exodus from the South that took place between 1910 and the late 1960s.

African Americans like Denham are returning to a region different from the segregationist South they left. Denham said the racial climate in Mississippi is "200 percent better" now than when he was growing up there. He thinks racial prejudice is more rampant now in the North.

William Frey, a demographer who teaches at SUNY Albany, said African Americans are being attracted to the South by a combination of economic, social and weather conditions. In addition to expatriates like Denham, the South is attracting many young African Americans, particularly college graduates, who were born and raised in the North, he said.

The migration pattern began reversing itself in the 1970s, according to Frey.

"That's when the economy in the industrial North started to go down the tubes," he said. "It also coincided with the beginning of the civil rights movement."

While Syracuse is losing some black residents to the South, its African-American population is still growing. U.S. Census Bureau figures show Central New York's African-American population grew from 43,052 in 1990 to 46,334 in 1998. That's a gain of 7.62 percent.

During the 1990s, booming "New South" cities saw tremendous growth in black population. Some of those cities, such as Atlanta and Charlotte, are also the top destinations for people leaving Central New York.

"For professional blacks, there's a fairly large black middle class in a place like Atlanta," Frey said.

The Rev. H. Bernard Alex, pastor of Second Olivet Baptist Church in Syracuse, has seen several members of his predominantly African American congregation relocate to the South in recent years.

"There is a sense of African-American mobility—economically and socially."
—Rev. H. Bernard Alex, pastor of Second Olivet Baptist Church

---

"There is a sense of African-American mobility—economically and socially," he said.

Places in the South once hostile to African Americans are now hospitable because they have African Americans in key leadership roles in law enforcement, education and business, he said.

Alex, a Syracuse native, went to Tuskegee University in Tuskegee, Ala.

"The one thing I noticed when I was in Alabama is that people are more upfront and honest if they have racial concerns and issues, more so than they are here," Alex said. "I can deal with that a lot better than the covert kind of stuff that happens in many instances in the Northern states."

But Alex sees a major drawback to the South's growth.

"Some of those cities are becoming so mega in size that a lot of the vices and issues that were once relegated to Chicago, Detroit, New York City and Newark are now right there in those same areas where they once never heard of such things," he said. "Here in Central New York, we have our challenges, but I feel a little more comfortable with my children here."

Bruce R. Hare, a professor of African-American studies and sociology at Syracuse University, said many African Americans have become disillusioned with the "paternalistic liberalism of the North."

"Racism in the North, while apparently a little more subtle and sophisticated, is no less real than in the South," Hare said. "The South may in fact bypass the North . . . in providing opportunities for African Americans."

Denham is content with the quality of life in Hickory, Miss. "It's a quiet little town," he said.

After he first returned to the South, Denham said he missed Syracuse for a year.

"I don't miss it at all now," he said. "Every time I go back up there to visit I stay about a week, then I'm ready to come back."

Where the Buffalo Roam, Again[5]

By Glen Martin
San Francisco Chronicle, April 22, 2001

Brian Meirs first noticed it a few years ago. The game was coming back.

It was subtle in the beginning—a few more sharp-tailed grouse along the section roads than usual, more deer peering from the margins of the hayfields at night. Then people started noticing there were larger numbers of pronghorn antelope than had ever been seen, and they were hanging around closer to town.

"Even 10 years ago, you never heard of mountain lion or elk around here," said Meirs, a state game warden who works the vast plains and mesa country around Buffalo. "Now they're pretty common. There are even occasional wolf sightings. It's like the wildlife was back there in the shadows, waiting for a change."

The change has been building for decades. The western Great Plains contain the country's greatest demographic anomaly: Its human population is emptying out. The trend, the 2000 census shows, has really gained force over the past decade with the drying up of the ranching economy.

But as people move away, wildlife is starting to fill the vacuum. In an unexpected way, a vision of the Great Plains as a wild commons is taking hold.

"It's funny—Buffalo Commons is really happening," Meirs said, as he sat in his truck on the main drag of Buffalo, a thoroughfare framed by abandoned storefronts. "Not like people thought it would. But it's happening."

The concept of the Buffalo Commons was floated by New Jersey sociologists Frank and Deborah Popper in 1988. The Poppers observed that agriculture had failed miserably on the Great Plains, and noted that the region would probably be almost wholly depopulated save for a few cities by the mid-21st century.

The highest and best use for the area, the Poppers argued, was in its pristine state: A restored prairie cleared of fences and abandoned ranches, reseeded with native bunchgrasses, teeming with wildlife. And foremost among these resurgent animals would be the emblematic beast of the Plains: the buffalo. Back by the tens, perhaps hundreds, of thousands.

Plains residents, both white and Native American, would earn their money through ecotourism and franchise hunting, not punching cows and growing dryland wheat.

Because the Poppers' proposal was predicated in part on federal buyouts of private property, it kicked off a howling storm of protest from the Great Plains agricultural

The depopulation affecting the region is . . . the dying of a dream.

community. Ranchers saw it as the most sinister possible example of a federal land grab. Resistance was so great that the idea died aborning.

But that didn't change the reality of Plains demographics—a reality best apprehended from the air.

Fly in a puddle jumper from Denver to Bismarck, N.D., and look down. There are great tracts of Badlands and rolling prairie, huge expanses of "pothole country" spangled with ponds and marshes, entire square miles of dryland wheat and irrigated alfalfa, serpentine brown rivers lined with cottonwoods, the occasional road. Very few ranches, and fewer towns. No cities.

The West and East coasts, the intermountain West, the Southwest, the Gulf Coast and the Deep South—they're exploding with development. Even the industrial Northeast, long a laggard in population growth, is gaining new people.

But not out here where the buffalo once roamed. Nearly three-quarters of Plains counties—322 of 443—have lost population since 1930. According to the 2000 census, 272 of 443 of the Plains counties have experienced population declines since 1990.

Demographers estimate that rural counties of the Dakotas could lose an additional third of their population in the next 20 years. From eastern New Mexico through the Texas and Oklahoma panhandles, to large portions of Colorado, Kansas, Nebraska, the Dakotas and Montana, the story is the same.

The depopulation affecting the region is nothing more than the dying of a dream. Or a scheme, at least. At the turn of the century, the western Plains were considered the globe's most promising emerging breadbasket.

Cattle had thrived on the rich prairie bunchgrasses after the subjugation of the Plains Indians and the elimination of the buffalo. Now, decided the pols in Washington, D.C., the rich black earth beneath the virgin sod would grow the nation's wheat.

The late 19th century and early 20th century were fairly wet on the prairie, reinforcing a popular idea of the time that "rain followed the plow." But years of drought followed, and homesteaders began washing out. The ruins of their farms are all over the Plains, ranging from abandoned dugout hovels to derelict three-story houses that are home to nothing but bats and owls.

"Agriculture around here is changing so fast you won't even recognize it in 10 years," said game warden Meirs as he sat in his truck listening to the wind whistle down Buffalo's main street. "The cattle and sheep are going by the wayside."

Buffalo Commons, it seems, is destined to occur—no matter what it's called, no matter who loves or hates it. But the forging of the Commons isn't a completely passive process.

True, the great federal investment envisioned by the Poppers didn't happen, nor is that likely. Given general public sentiment against extravagant government spending programs, it's inconceivable that Congress would loosen up the purse strings to fund the purchase of tens of millions of acres of bankrupt rangeland.

"Agriculture around here is changing so fast you won't even recognize it in 10 years."— **Brian Meirs, game warden**

Instead, Buffalo Commons is becoming a private enterprise. And leading the movement is media mogul Ted Turner, who appears to have made the North American bison his private totem. Turner owns about 1.7 million acres divided among several ranches scattered across the Plains, and that figure is growing.

"I heard tell that Ted Turner wants to be able to ride all the way from Canada to Mexico on his own land," drawled one Nebraska rancher. "And the way he's going, it isn't going to be too long before he can do that."

Turner looks for a certain kind of property: One that's in grass rather than croplands, with natural contours intact. He wants good biodiversity—country that supports substantial populations of wildlife of numerous species.

And when he buys properties, he more or less follows the same formula: Tear out all the cross fencing and replant pastures with bunchgrasses and other native vegetation. Bring in the buffalo.

Turner believes that ranching can be profitable on the Plains—but not necessarily by raising cattle. He's promoting the sale of buffalo breeding stock and meat, luxury big game and bird hunts and ecotourism tours as the economic saviors of the region.

Unlike many celebrity landowners, Turner isn't gate-happy, and doesn't seem to mind rubberneckers as long as they don't stop to shoot his buffalo.

Black-tailed Prairie Dogs Struggle
for Home on Range

Bison are generally considered the emblematic animal of the Great Plains, and reintroduction efforts for the shaggy beasts are almost universally popular.

But there's another keystone Plains species essential to grasslands restoration—and it's not nearly as esteemed as the buffalo.

Prairie dogs were once the most common mammal in North America. In the late 19th century, about five billion prairie dogs of five species inhabited the Plains from Canada to Mexico. The vast majority were black-tailed prairie dogs, a stocky, buff-colored rodent that weighs between two to three pounds.

Their vast towns comprised complete ecologies in their own right: One in Texas measured 100 miles wide, 250 miles long and contained an estimated 400 million dogs.

Prairie dogs shaped the Plains as much as the buffalo, and a considerable array of wild species depended on the rodents for shelter and food.

The prairie dogs' various diggings provide shelter for a great many animals: badgers, foxes, burrowing owls and a tremendous variety of reptiles, amphibians and insects.

The huge quantity of feces and urine produced by the dog towns was a gigantic fertilizing mechanism for the Plains.

Today, prairie dogs only inhabit about 1 percent of their former range; the black-tailed prairie dog is a candidate for protection under the U.S. Endangered Species Act. Their decline began shortly after cattlemen moved to the Plains. Seen as competitors with cattle for forage, the dogs were poisoned and shot out.

A coalition of environmentalists is agitating for a return of the dog.

"Prairie dogs are decreasing in numbers across their range," said Jonathan Proctor, a program associate with the Predator Coalition Alliance in Bozeman, Mont.

Proctor's group was able to secure a temporary ban on poisoning on federal lands through a petition to list black-tailed prairie dogs under the U.S. Endangered Species Act.

But the dogs are still shot in large numbers, often for sport. Such activities are widely condoned by ranchers.

"There's no shortage of prairie dogs," said South Dakota rancher Pat Clark, who said the animals compete with cattle for grass and endanger livestock with their burrows. "They're all over the place."

But scattered families of prairie dogs are no indication of the general health of the five species, Proctor said.

Despite the pressures facing prairie dogs, Proctor said he is guardedly optimistic about their future.

Colorado recently banned sport hunting for black-tailed prairie dogs, and South Dakota and Montana are considering similar restrictions, said Proctor.

"Basically, they'll come back if we stop actively killing them," he said.

And there are plenty of buffalo to see. Under a sky crowded with lowering gray cumulus, a couple of hundred of the shaggy beasts grazed near a roadside. About a mile away, on the same vast tract of rolling prairie, a similar number fed.

A Lakota hunter could have witnessed precisely this scene in this same place 150 years ago.

And buffalo aren't the only animals thriving on Turner's property. Big coveys of sharp-tailed grouse fly unhurriedly out of the way at the approach of a truck. White-tailed deer bolt from every coulee. Stop to watch scores of blue-winged teal bank and swoop around a pothole, and you catch the eerie, wild yapping of two coyotes singing in antiphony in the distance.

Although he is operating on the most ambitious scale, Turner is by no means the only New Age buffalo rancher on the Plains. Many of Turner's compeers don't necessarily share his wildlife habitat goals. But the wildlife is nevertheless reaping the benefits of their bison husbandry.

Kirk Budd, the proprietor of Freshwater Ranch in Nebraska's Sand Hills, has lived the quintessential hardscrabble Plains life. He raised cattle until "they just about starved me out." He was a bush pilot in Canada for years, and was a crop duster until a pesticide accident almost killed him.

Things, in short, were looking pretty grim for Budd. He was in danger of busting out, losing his ranch. Then a few years ago, he bought some buffalo.

"They were cheap then," recalled Budd, crawling out from under an airplane he was repairing at his ranch. "About $400 for a cow. So I figured what the heck."

Budd gradually expanded his herd, keeping the heifer calves, selling the bulls. He now owns several hundred buffalo on three ranches totaling 11,000 acres. Many are verging on coal black, and all are huge—much darker and far larger than Turner's brown-and-russet buffalo. His bred heifers sell for about $4,000.

Although Budd doesn't believe bison will utterly supplant cattle on the Plains, he feels buffalo ranching will continue to grow.

"The National Buffalo Association says the country's herds are growing at 12 percent a year, but I know it's more than that. I know a lot of people in this business, and everyone is keeping all their heifers. I figure the real figure is more like 40 percent a year."

And compared with cattle, buffalo have been good to his land, Budd notes. Cattle like to wallow in water, tearing up creeks and ponds and trampling vegetation. But buffalo associate water with predators. They all go down at once to drink, then get out right away to higher ground. The creeks stay vegetated, and the water stays clean.

Indeed, the Freshwater Ranch looks markedly different from neighboring properties where cattle are grazed. The forage is in better condition, and the streams and ponds are far more vegetated. A creek that runs by the ranch house looks like prime trout water, and Budd confirms it is full of large brown trout.

And the ranch burgeons with wildlife.

"A lot of critters like being with buffalo," Budd said. "They evolved with them. Deer, elk, antelope, wild turkeys. We even have bighorn sheep on one of our ranches. You can ranch buffalo, maybe even tame some you raise from a bottle. But they're basically wildlife. And you can see that reflected in the condition of the range on any ranch where they're raised."

As bullish as he is on buffalo, Budd doesn't think much of Buffalo Commons.

"That will never, never fly out here," he said. "As soon as you start talking big government involvement, people resist. Also, a lot of this land is still irrigated, particularly to the east of the Sand Hills. It's growing soybeans, wheat, corn and alfalfa.

"As a general policy, I don't think you should take all that food land out of production for a wildlife park. That's just not good for the nation."

While Plains farmers resist government intervention, they do understand—and appreciate—government subsidies.

Federal payouts have been part of America's ranching and farming culture for decades, and although they have diminished in recent years, they're still relied on to make ends meet.

> *"As soon as you start talking big government involvement, people resist."*
> —**Kirk Budd, proprietor of Freshwater Ranch**

Since the mid-1980s, many of those subsidies have been paid to cattle ranchers to conserve wildlife habitat on their lands. In the Dakotas, almost 500,000 acres of upland and wetland habitat have been preserved under these conservation reserve programs, benefiting a variety of species, but particularly migratory waterfowl.

The coteau region—a vast, hilly stretch of glacially carved potholes and ponds in the Dakotas, eastern Montana, Saskatchewan and Alberta—is a duck factory, explained Scott McCleod, a biologist with the northern Plains regional office of Ducks Unlimited in Bismarck.

Ducks Unlimited is a conservation organization composed of primarily hunters that preserve wetlands and grasslands prairie. So far, it has saved 8 million acres of habitat essential to waterfowl in the United States and Canada.

"Sixty to 70 percent of the continent's major duck species breed in the prairie pothole region," McCleod said. "During the winter and spring migrations, the potholes serve as critical resting and staging areas for the birds."

The historic temptation for farmers, McCleod said, has been to drain the potholes to increase tillable acreage and plow the grass for relatively profitable crops like wheat, corn and sunflowers.

"That's why we like to work with cattle ranchers rather than farmers," said McCleod. "Ranchers are interested in the same thing we are—preserving the grasslands."

The restoration under way is not necessarily a process that will proceed smoothly and steadily. Federal funds for conservation reserve programs could dry up; a prolonged recession could make the buying of megaranches by conservation-minded billionaires like Turner a thing of the past.

But nothing, it seems, will change the bedrock reality of the western Plains: They are not well-suited for agriculture or year-round human habitation.

Returning Species of the Great Plains

Bison. The emblem of the Plains, and a growing commercial alternative to beef. More buffalo are living now than at any time since the 19th century.

Sharp-tailed grouse. A large game bird that has responded well to grassland restoration efforts. Performs elaborate mating dances in spring.

Pronghorn antelope. Ubiquitous throughout the western Plains. Flashes white rump patches when alarmed. Often seen grazing near cattle or bison.

Black-footed ferret. North America's rarest predator. Associated with prairie dog colonies.

Leopard frog. Instantly recognizable, leopard frogs have declined over much of their range, but are doing well in large tracts of undisturbed prairie pothole country.

Black-tailed prairie dog. An architect of Plains ecology. Greatly diminished in range, but efforts are under way to re-establish "dog towns" on both federal refuges and private ranches.

Native Americans knew how to live on them—by passing through, by following the buffalo that peregrinated from horizon to horizon.

The record of permanent settlement on the Plains, on the other hand, has been dismal. One way or another, the Plains will devolve to their earlier condition: To a sea of grass, where people are the transient visitors, wildlife the enduring residents.

IV. How We Live Now

Figure 9

Households by Size: Selected Years, 1970 to 2000
(Percent distribution)

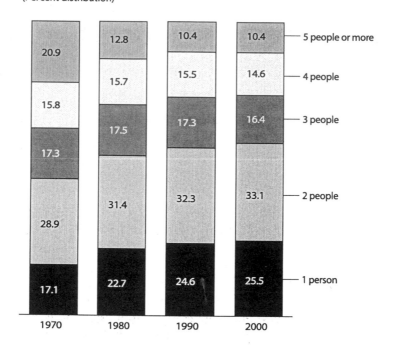

Figure 10

Households by Type: Selected Years, 1970 to 2000
(Percent distribution)

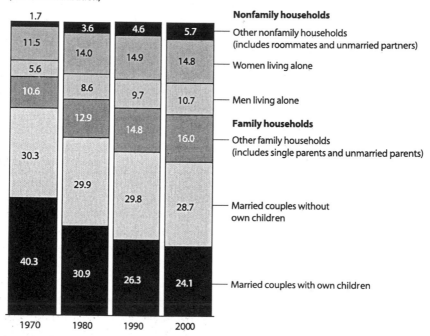

Source: U.S. Census Bureau, Current Population Survey, March Supplements: 1970 to 2000.

Editor's Introduction

Next to the jump in the Latino population, the census data that have attracted the most attention (and, in some cases, loud cries of shock and horror) have been the statistics about the American family. As the articles in this section indicate, the so-called "traditional" household of the past has evolved into something very different.

Eric Schmitt summarizes those figures, which are a source of concern for so many, in "For the First Time, Nuclear Families Drop Below 25% of Households," though he explains that some of the numbers may not actually be as alarming as they look. In part, they simply reflect an economy that allows more young people and more senior citizens to maintain households of their own, as well as the aging of the "baby boomers," whose older offspring, now in their twenties, are moving out to live on their own. It is important, in gazing at the numbers, not to lose sight of the natural occurrences of ordinary life. Nevertheless, as Schmitt suggests, the sense of what is "ordinary" may be changing. Even taking into consideration the factors mentioned above, the 2000 census shows a declining percentage of married couples with children and a steady increase in unmarried couples living together, often with children, and in families headed by a single parent. No one is sure what to make of the single-parent/unmarried parents trend, but it worries almost everybody, mainly because the children involved would seem to have less stability in their lives. The fact that a disproportionate number of single-parent families are living at or below the poverty line adds to the general uneasiness.

On a more hopeful note, the 2000 census also uncovered an unexpected number of households that extend to three generations, one of several developments discussed in D'Vera Cohn and Sarah Cohen's wide-ranging article "Census Sees Vast Change in Language, Employment," from the *Washington Post*. The 2000 census was the first ever to collect statistics about grandparents—those living with their children and grandchildren, and those raising their grandchildren alone. Such arrangements have turned out to be more common than demographers had thought. In the future these households may receive more attention from legislators and from social services.

Another surprise has been a sudden increase in the tiny percentage of households that consist of same-sex partners, as reported by Lee Condon in "By the Numbers." Although the census asks no questions about sexual preferences, starting in 1990 it did offer gay and lesbian couples who live together (with or without children) the option of identifying themselves as unmarried partners. Very few people availed themselves of that option in 1990, but in 2000 the number tripled, reaching one-half of one percent of households nationwide. These households were also broadly distributed, occurring in all but 55 of America's counties. Demographers interpret this as evidence of a change in social attitudes toward greater tolerance, and a corresponding increase of confidence among gay and lesbian couples.

Finally, in "Poverty Rates Fell in 2000, But Income Was Stagnant," Katharine Q. Seelye reports on the early statistics about income for that year released by the Census Bureau. Although detailed information on the entire decade will not be forthcoming until 2002, it is already clear that the economic boom of the 1990s is over, and that it benefitted some much more than others. A decline in economic prospects may affect many families in the decade ahead, leading to further changes in living arrangements. What those will be remains to be seen.

For the First Time, Nuclear Families Drop Below 25% of Households[1]

BY ERIC SCHMITT
NEW YORK TIMES, MAY 15, 2001

For the first time, less than a quarter of the households in the United States are made up of married couples with their children, new census data show.

That results from a number of factors, like many men and women delaying both marriage and having children, more couples living longer after their adult children leave home and the number of single-parent families growing much faster than the number of married couples.

Indeed, the number of families headed by women who have children, which are typically poorer than two-parent families, grew nearly five times faster in the 1990s than the number of married couples with children, a trend that some family experts and demographers described today as disturbing.

The new data offer the 2000 census' first glimpse into the shifting and complicated makeup of American families and carry wide-ranging implications that policy makers and politicians are already struggling to address.

With more communities having fewer households with children, public schools often face an increasingly difficult time gathering support for renovating aging buildings and investing in education over all. Voters in Cleveland last week approved $380 million in levies to fix city schools, but only after two months of exhaustive lobbying by civic leaders.

"This may have something to do with why our education system is not up to snuff," said Isabel Sawhill, a senior fellow at the Brookings Institution. "Oftentimes, those parents who still are invested in the schools don't have the money or influence to change things."

Demographers expressed surprise that the number of unmarried couples in the United States nearly doubled in the 1990s, to 5.5 million couples from 3.2 million in 1990. Some of those couples have children.

Many conservative groups point to the increase as well as the statistics on single-parent households as troubling indicators of deeper societal problems.

"This data shows we need to regain the importance of marriage as a social institution," said Bridget Maher, a marriage and family policy analyst at the conservative Family Research Council. "People are disregarding the importance of marriage and the importance of having a mother and father who are married."

Ms. Maher and other conservatives point to the findings as justification for the enactment of policies that they say would strengthen the family, like eliminating the so-called marriage penalty in the tax code.

> *"Being married is great, but being married with kids is tougher in today's society."*
> **—William H. Frey, University of Michigan**

The decades-long decline in the overall number of American households with children slowed during the 1990s as two of the most troubling trends—divorce and out-of-wedlock births—moderated, demographers said.

But even with that slowdown, the percentage of married-couple households with children under 18 has declined to 23.5 percent of all households in 2000 from 25.6 percent in 1990, and from 45 percent in 1960, said Martin O'Connell, chief of the Census Bureau's fertility and family statistics branch. The number of Americans living alone, 26 percent of all households, surpassed, for the first time, the number of married-couple households with children.

William H. Frey, a demographer at the University of Michigan, said, "Being married is great, but being married with kids is tougher in today's society with spouses in different jobs and expensive day care and schools."

The number of married-couple families with children grew by just under 6 percent in the 1990s. In contrast, households with children headed by single mothers, which account for nearly 7 percent of all households, increased by 25 percent in the 1990s.

The new census data paint a more detailed picture of the American family in other ways.

Unmarried couples represent 9 percent of all unions, up from 6 percent a decade ago.

"It's certainly consistent with what we've all been noting, the growth in cohabitation in this country, but it also tells us how complex American families are becoming," said Freya L. Sonenstein, director of population studies at the Urban Institute in Washington and a visiting fellow at the Public Policy Institute of California.

The number of non-family households, which consist of people living alone or with people who are not related, make up about one-third of all households. They grew at twice the rate of family households in the 1990s.

Demographers pointed to several factors to explain the figures. People are marrying later, if they marry at all. The median age of the first marriage for men has increased to 27 years old from 22 in 1960; for women, it has increased to 25 years old from 20 in 1960, said Campbell Gibson, a Census Bureau demographic adviser.

The booming economy has allowed more younger people to leave home and live on their own. Divorce, while leveling off, has left many middle-age people living alone—at least temporarily. Advances in medicine and bulging stock portfolios have permitted many elderly people to live independently longer.

"It's easier for a young person to start out on his own or live in a group home," said Mr. O'Connell. "And the elderly population is healthier and economically better off."

Census officials said the median age of the country's population increased to 35.3 years old, the highest it has ever been. This reflects the influence of the so-called baby boom generation, born between 1946 and 1964. The most rapid increase in size of any age group was the 49 percent jump in the population 45-to-54 years old.

While an influx of immigrants and other foreign-born residents with larger, younger families held down this aging indicator, several other statistics underscore the demographic and marketing power the baby boomers wield as they enter their peak earning years. For example, the share of owner-occupied housing increased to 66 percent in 2000 compared with 64 percent in 1990.

"Baby boomers are driving the increase in owner-occupied housing," said Jeffrey S. Passel, a demographer at the Urban Institute, a social policy research organization. "Ten years from now, they will be pushing pre-retirement homes, and 20 years from now they will cause the Social Security crisis."

The new census data also show that while there are still about 5 million more women than men in the United States, men are narrowing the gap partly because of improved medicine and greater health awareness by men, but also because of slightly higher rates of lung-related deaths among women, primarily due to increased smoking among them, demographers said.

The number of men for every 100 women increased to 96.3 in 2000 from 95.1 in 1990, largely because men are closing the life-expectancy gap with women. As of 1998, the latest figures available from the National Center for Health Statistics, women on average live 79.5 years, up from 78.8 years in 1990.

Men can expect to live 73.8 years, up from 71.8 years in 1990, Mr. Gibson said.

Within the refined demographic profile, there were also intriguing trends among specific racial groups. For instance, the overall Asian population in the United States grew by 48 percent in the 1990s, but the number of Chinese, Indians and Vietnamese doubled or nearly doubled in the decade.

Census Sees Vast Change in Language, Employment[2]

By D'Vera Cohn and Sarah Cohen
Washington Post, August 6, 2001

The most detailed demographic snapshot in a decade describes a nation where nearly 1 in 5 Americans does not speak English at home, more than 2 million grandparents are raising their grandchildren, and the number of adults who work solely out of their homes has grown a third since 1990.

The statistics released by the U.S. Census Bureau today offer telling evidence of broad social and economic forces shaping the country: immigration, new technologies and a dramatic diversification of family life. The number of children whose mothers hold jobs while their fathers do not, for example, is up 70 percent compared with a decade ago.

The numbers come from a national survey of 700,000 households, conducted in conjunction with the 2000 census, and touch on a vast array of topics, from housing costs to occupations and commuting patterns. Because the survey asked questions similar to those on the census, it is viewed by demographers as the first look at the most detailed information that will be released next year. Unlike the door-to-door head count, however, it does not include college dormitories, prisons, military barracks and other "group quarters."

Described broadly, the information portrays a nation in transformation, although the trends are sometimes contradictory. Quality of life is rising for many U.S. residents. Yet 1 in 6 children lives in poverty, the numbers show, and a growing share of the population struggles with English.

Overall, Americans are better-housed and better-educated than they were 10 years ago. Fewer homes lack plumbing, telephones or cars. Fewer are crowded. The number of households with three or more cars grew 20 percent.

One in four Americans age 25 or older has a bachelor's degree, up from 1 in 5 a decade earlier. But the figure is much higher in the District [of Columbia], where about 4 in 10 adults are college-educated.

---

2. Copyright © 2001, *The Washington Post*. Reprinted with permission.

The new figures, available for the nation as a whole and the 50 states and the District individually, point to differences between the capital and the country. The District, for example, ranks third behind California and New York in the share of residents who spend 40 percent or more of their income on housing.

Reflecting its urban character, the District also ranks at the top in residents who do not own a vehicle—37 percent. Information for local suburban counties will be available next month.

The statistics, combined with earlier results of the census, underscore the extent to which U.S. families are changing, with children increasingly likely to live with single mothers and unmarried couples. For the first time, the Census Bureau has tallied how many grandparents are raising their grandchildren.

> ***"The real surprise was the extremely large proportion of grandparents who are raising their grandchildren."*—Martin O'Connell, chief of the Census Bureau's Fertility and Family Statistics Branch**

That question was mandated in the 1996 welfare reform law, as lawmakers and welfare officials warned of the number of parents unable to care for their children because they were addicted to drugs, in prison or dead.

The survey found that 3.2 million grandparents live with grandchildren for whom they are not primary caretakers and an additional 2 million live with grandchildren under 18 for whom they are responsible.

"This is a dramatic example of how multi-generational connections are becoming more important in American society," said Vern Bengston, a gerontology professor at the University of Southern California. "Grandparents are helping more than ever before."

Bengston describes these grandparents as part of a larger intergenerational revolution underway in American society.

"That's probably the most dramatic example of unplanned parenthood I can think of," he said.

Of the grandparents primarily responsible for their grandchildren's care, most are married and most hold a job, the census figures show. Most are not poor.

"The real surprise was the extremely large proportion of grandparents who are doing this . . . for three, four, five years or more," said Martin O'Connell, chief of the Census Bureau's Fertility and Family Statistics Branch. "It's clearly a situation where this is really a growing and developing family."

Grandparents and their advocates hope the numbers will help them push for laws to make it easier to gain custody of a neglected or abused grandchild. Without custody, it is difficult to deal with schools or doctors, and impossible to obtain subsidized health insurance or day care, if needed.

Donna Butts, executive director of Generations United, a national nonprofit advocacy group, said the publication of the number "really is acknowledging that this is a family unit in our country that is deserving of recognition."

Eleanor Simpson, who is raising a great-grandchild and two grandchildren in her Rockville home, stays afloat by baby-sitting and receiving some government assistance. She took in the children when one mother died and another had drug problems. Simpson asked to be identified by her maiden name because she has more people living with her than her lease allows.

"Sometimes I don't think I am doing a great job at all," she said. "I wonder how we made it through. The best part of the whole thing is the love you get from your grandchildren."

Pat Owens, of Frederick County, who is raising two grandchildren and is active in the grandparents' rights movement, said the experience has changed her priorities.

"We just get up and go until we can't go anymore," she said. "I don't do housework anymore. We don't sweat the small stuff."

The census figures also document both a growing number of foreign-born Americans and a growing share who speak little or no English. The nation gained more immigrants in the 1990s than in any previous decade. Demographer Steven Camarota, with the Center for Immigration Studies, said his calculations indicate that immigrants—and births to immigrants—account for most U.S. population growth over the decade.

Not only are more U.S. residents reporting that they do not speak English at home, more than 10.5 million said they speak little or no English. That is up from 6.5 million in 1990.

Nearly one-third of them live in California, where 1 in 9 people over age 5 has limited English proficiency, according to the survey. Locally, nearly 18,000 people in the District reported that they speak little or no English. So did nearly 107,000 in Maryland and more than 125,000 in Virginia; in both states, most immigrants live in the Washington suburbs.

Some of the rise, experts say, is due to the fast growth of the new-immigrant population, which included millions of people who came here illegally.

"If someone is here for a short time or someone is here illegally, the incentive to learn English is less than someone who has tried hard and achieved legal permanent residence," said Guillermina Jasso, sociology professor at New York University.

The share of people who speak little English is highest among those in their working years, ages 18 to 64.

"The elementary school kids are getting much more attention to their needs than the high school students," said Jeffrey S. Passel, an Urban Institute researcher. "The adults are problematic."

Even as the economy welcomed more new immigrants, it also fed the growth of the nation's work-at-home population. Technology and a freelance economy made it possible. Sprawl and traffic congestion made it desirable.

The number of Americans who work from home rose by nearly 1 million over the decade, reaching 4 million, the survey said. But that figure is a vast underestimate of the number who work at home, Census Bureau officials said, because it includes only people who never go into the office.

"We feel sure we missed people who worked at home one or two days, but went to the office other days," said Philip Salopek, the Census Bureau's top commuting expert.

The work-at-home population has always been largest in rural states, but it dropped over the decade in such places as South Dakota, Iowa and Nebraska, where the farm economy is shrinking. Numbers rose most sharply in Washington state, Hawaii, Florida, Georgia, South Carolina, Delaware and the District.

The census figures also illustrate changing gender roles: The number of children living with both parents but only the mother working rose significantly, from 1 million in 1990 to 1.7 million in 2000.

Some fathers in those homes are going to school; others are disabled or retired; and some are stay-at-home dads by choice.

Pete Baylies, who has published a newsletter for at-home dads from his house in suburban Boston since 1993, credits articles and movies about fathers like himself with contributing to an atmosphere of greater acceptance. At-home dads feel less awkward now.

"Twenty or 30 years ago, they were almost freakish," he said. "Now, when they go to the playground, mothers don't look at them with as much doubt as they used to."

By the Numbers[3]

By Lee Condon
Advocate, September 25, 2001

Census 2000 may be best remembered as the gay census. For the first time, federal head-counters made a real effort to enumerate gay and lesbian households. As the data were released—four or five states a time—the numbers made the front pages of newspapers in big cities and small towns throughout the country. Although single gays and lesbians were left out of the count, demographers say the tally of 1.2 million same-sex "unmarried partners" is the result of the most substantial polling ever to be done of gays and lesbians in America.

While a study commissioned by the gay lobby group the Human Rights Campaign estimates that Census 2000 undercounted gay and lesbian couples by a huge 62%, the data nevertheless show that gays and lesbians are living in 99.3% of all counties in the United States.

"It's extremely important in the sense that gays and lesbians are the subject of an enormous amount of public policy discussions," says Gary Gates, a research associate at the Urban Institute, which conducted a study on the census commissioned by the Human Rights Campaign. "In most cases these policies have been debated with no information [about] how many people are affected by them."

HRC spokesman David Smith agrees. "What this does for the country is it changes the debate," he says. "It turns it into a debate about real people and real families."

Much was made of the massive increase in the number of same-sex couples in the past decade when the first statistics for 2000 were released this spring. Nationwide, the number of people reporting themselves as same-sex unmarried partners went up 314%. In Wyoming the increase was an astounding 2,590%.

But by the time numbers for the final states were reported in mid August, census officials were saying it wasn't appropriate to compare 1990 data to that from 2000. The Census Bureau now acknowledges that there were flaws in how it classified gay and lesbian households in 1990. At that time, in most cases where same-sex cou-

---

3. Article by Lee Condon from *The Advocate*, September 25, 2001. Copyright © 2001 by Lee Condon. Reprinted with permission.

ples identified themselves as married, the bureau changed the sex of one of the partners. Therefore, many same-sex households were counted as heterosexual ones.

In 2000 the bureau reclassified such couples as "unmarried partners."

But HRC officials say the 2000 figures still represent an undercount. They cite several tallies that suggest the number of gay couples in the United States is much higher than the 601,000 (1.2 million gay and lesbian individuals) included in the census..

In his analysis, Gates says other sources suggest a much higher number of gay couples. While the census shows gay people in same-sex couple households represent less than 1% of the U.S. population, exit polls by Voter News Service in the last three elections registered the gay vote at between 4% and 5%. If 5% of the total U.S. adult population of 209 million were gay, there would be 10.4 million gay people in the United States.

A recent study of gay and lesbian voting habits conducted by Harris Interactive determined that 30% of gay and lesbian people are living together in committed relationships. Using those figures,

---

Gay-Friendly

Top 10 counties ranked by percentage of coupled households that are gay or lesbian

1.	San Francisco County, Calif.	6.91%
2.	District of Columbia	5.14%
3.	New York County, N.Y.	4.34%
4.	Suffolk County, Mass.	3.55%
5.	Arlington County, Va.	3.13%
6.	DeKalb County, Ga.	2.97%
7.	Denver County, Colo.	2.95%
8.	Alexandria County, Va.	2.93%
9.	Monroe County, Fla.	2.86%
10.	Hampshire County, Mass.	2.8%

Gay-Free

Counties that have no recorded gay or lesbian couples

Colorado: Cheyenne and Hinsdale
Hawaii: Kalawao
Idaho: Oneida
Nebraska: Arthur, Blaine, Boyd, Greeley, Hayes, Hooker, Logan, Loup, Webster, and Wheeler
Montana: Liberty
North Dakota: Hettinger and Slope
Oklahoma: Cimarron
South Dakota: Buffalo
Texas: Kenedy, Loving, and Roberts

Gates suggests that there are actually 3.1 million gay and lesbian couples who live together in the United States, a figure that indicates the census under-counted gays by 62%.

But it's not entirely the Census Bureau's fault. Smith says many gay people are still afraid to identify themselves as such on a federal survey—even though identifying information is not released. Such fears are understandable in a country "where you can be fired for being gay, where you're not allowed to serve in the military and you're not allowed to be a Boy Scout," he says.

Another problem with tracking people based on their sexual orientation has to do with the fluidity of sexuality itself, Gates says. "Is being gay or lesbian being attracted to a member of the same sex? Or is it only people who actually have sex with members of their own sex?" he asks. "Does it include people who only sometimes have sex with members of their own sex?"

Nevertheless, Smith and others are advocating that the bureau for the first time ask a direct question about sexual orientation in Census 2010. And despite the problems that he and Gates acknowledge will accompany any attempt to truly measure the number of gay men and lesbians in the United States, they agree that the majority of people would be more than happy to answer such a question truthfully. In 2000, Gates says, most gay people simply "felt proud that they could finally document themselves in the census."

Where the Lesbians Are

In most states, gay male couples and lesbian couples are represented in almost equal numbers—the remarkable exception being Washington, D.C., where gay male couples make up 73% of the reported same-sex couples. But there are four states that lesbians seem to prefer. Ranked by the percentage of lesbian couples out of total same-sex couples reported, those states are:

Vermont	61% lesbian
Alaska	59% lesbian
New Mexico	58% lesbian
Oregon	57% lesbian

Poverty Rates Fell in 2000, But Income Was Stagnant[4]

By Katharine Q. Seelye
NEW YORK TIMES, SEPTEMBER 26, 2001

New economic statistics show that poverty in the United States declined in 2000, with the poverty rates of blacks and female heads of households the lowest on record. At the same time, median income has leveled off after years of growth.

The new figures, released today by the Census Bureau, showed that the median household income in 2000 was $42,148, adjusted for inflation—a shade off the record high reached in 1999 ($42,187 in 2000 dollars). Only the Northeast showed a statistical gain in income, up 3.9 percent to $45,106.

Median household income among Hispanics and blacks set records ($33,447 for Hispanics, $30,439 for blacks), with the income of blacks rising $1,600 from 1999. The median income for blacks was $15,000 lower than the median income for whites.

"This shows the continuing remarkable success of welfare reform," said Robert Rector, an analyst at the Heritage Foundation, a conservative research group. "There's been a dramatic drop in dependence."

The figures showed that the number of people in poverty had dropped, to 31.1 million in 2000 from 32.3 million in 1999. For a family of four, an annual income below $17,603 qualified them as impoverished; for one person, the poverty line was $8,794.

The poverty rate fell as well, for the fourth consecutive year, from 11.8 percent in 1999 to 11.3 percent in 2000, the lowest since 1979 and about the same as the lowest poverty rate ever recorded (11.1 percent in 1973).

However, analysts say, the average poor person fell further below the poverty line in 1999 and 2000 than in any other year since record-keeping began in 1979. They attributed the drop to cuts in food stamps and cash-assistance programs and to declining participation in those programs.

---

4. Article by Katharine Q. Seelye from *New York Times* September 26, 2001. Copyright © *New York Times*. Reprinted with permission.

The figures are based on a survey of 50,000 households in 2000 and do not reflect the recent rise in unemployment or other indicators that the economy was softening in the months before the terrorist attacks of September 11.

"The economy was clearly weakening before September 11, and that added another swift kick," said Robert Greenstein, executive director of the Center on Budget and Policy Priorities, a liberal research group.

> *"I was surprised, frankly, that household income was stagnant in 2000."*—Jared **Bernstein, Economic Policy Institute**

"It's too early to know if this is a mild, short-lasting downturn or whether the positive period of the '90s has ended and the downturn will be deeper and the rate of growth slower," Mr. Greenstein said.

He said it could take years to recover to the highs of 1999 and 2000. After the earlier peak prosperity year of 1989, poverty was never as low again until 1998 and income was never as high until 1996.

Mr. Greenstein and other analysts were puzzled about why the median income in 2000 remained unchanged from 1999, given low unemployment.

"I was surprised, frankly, that household income was stagnant in 2000," said Jared Bernstein, a senior economist at the Economic Policy Institute, a liberal research group. "So many other indicators were positive, one would have expected middle-income families to get their share of the growth, but that didn't happen."

Not only did income remain stagnant, but the earnings of men who worked full time dropped by a full percentage point, to $37,339 in 2000, the first time in four years that men experienced a decline.

The earnings of women were statistically unchanged, at $27,355. Women earned 73 cents to each dollar earned by men.

The household incomes of Asian-Americans and Pacific Islanders continued to be higher than those of other Americans, as they have since this group's income began being recorded by the Census Bureau in 1987, although they showed no significant increase in 2000 over 1999. Asian-Americans and Pacific Islanders had an average median income in 2000 of $55,521, compared with $45,904 for non-Hispanic whites (this is the only category that does not include Hispanics), $44,226 for whites, $33,447 for Hispanics and $30,439 for blacks.

Analysts said that most gains in income had been among high-income households and that the income gap between high income earners and lower-income earners remained at a post-World War II high.

"We still have an economy with very impressive opportunities for those at the top and not for those at the bottom," Mr. Bernstein said. "Yes, low-income families are working more and may have crossed the poverty line, but they are still near-poor. We have structural imbalances in our economy leading to ever-higher levels of inequality, and this boom hasn't cured that problem."

V. Reapportionment and Redistricting

Figure 11

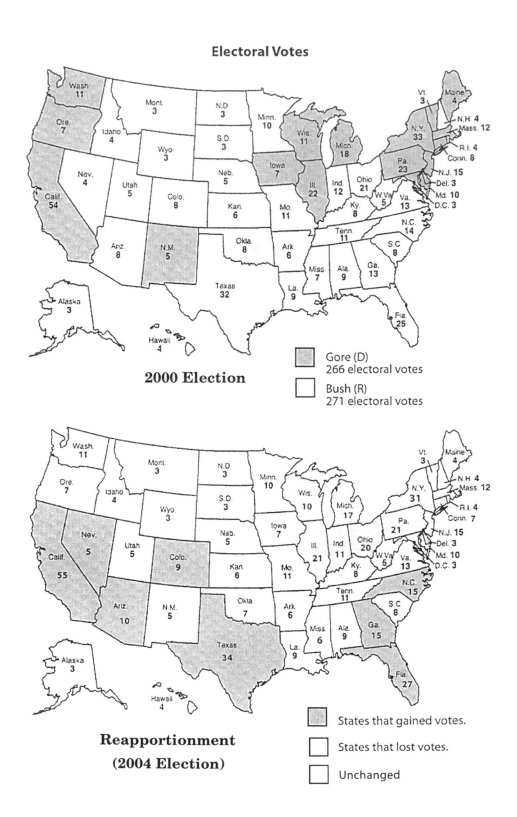

Electoral Votes

Gore (D)
266 electoral votes

Bush (R)
271 electoral votes

2000 Election

States that gained votes.

States that lost votes.

Unchanged

Reapportionment
(2004 Election)

Editor's Introduction

Whatever attractions the census may hold for demographers, sociologists, and curious students of the American scene, it has only one Constitutional purpose: to determine the composition of the House of Representatives. Each member of the House is supposed to represent approximately the same number of people, so states that make dramatic gains in population are usually entitled to additional seats in Congress (and additional votes in the Electoral College), while states that have grown more slowly are likely to lose a representative or two. (There are only 435 seats in total, and they have to be assigned according to the numbers.) Reapportionment takes place after every census; after the 2000 census, twelve seats were reassigned: New York and Pennsylvania each lost two, and Connecticut, Ohio, Illinois, Indiana, Michigan, Wisconsin, Oklahoma, and Mississippi each lost one. Among those that gained seats, Arizona, Texas, Georgia, and Florida won two apiece, while North Carolina, Colorado, Nevada, and California each received one.

At first glance, the drift of population away from states that voted for Gore in the 2000 election and toward western and southern states that mostly voted for Bush would seem to promise a bonanza for the Republican party. But this is not necessarily the case. Who wins and who loses in a local election may very well depend on where the district lines are drawn. Redistricting follows reapportionment and involves changing the boundaries of election districts to reflect the latest statistics. Redistricting is absolutely necessary whenever a state gains or loses a seat in Congress and is often required even when there is no change in state representation, to account for shifts of population within the state. For sheer hardball politics, nothing beats it. Under the guise of seeking a fair apportionment, each party will try to draw district lines in a way that will minimize the opposition's impact, perhaps by splitting up opposition voters among several different districts or by "packing" them all into one district, leaving a clear field elsewhere. Under the Voting Rights Act of 1965, passed when newly registered African Americans were being gerrymandered into majority-white districts, it became illegal to alter district boundaries in ways clearly meant to dilute the voting strength of a minority. This somewhat limits the number of backroom games that can be played; however, it increases the number of lawsuits that can be filed.

In "Gerrymandering for Position in 2002," Joshua Green provides an overview of the process and explains why both parties see opportunities for advancement. Suzanne Dougherty's piece, "Connecticut Prepares to Sacrifice a Seat," describes a classic situation. One (but which one?) of the state's six representatives is about to be redistricted out of a job and will be forced to retire or to run against an entrenched incumbent in the congressional election of 2002. Since the state's delegation is now evenly divided between Republicans and Democrats, this is a matter of great concern to both parties.

Minority voters are expected to play an important role in future local contests. Several commentators have noted that if the Hispanic and black minorities worked together, they could exercise considerable political influence. However, although the two groups have a common agenda on some issues, such as education, they are far apart on others, such as immigration. In "Race to be 'Largest' Puts Minority Groups in Last Place," Julianne Malveaux issues an angry call for unity. Daniel B. Wood then describes the situation in multiracial Los Angeles, where an expanding Latino population seeks a greater role in local government and sometimes finds itself competing with other minorities, in "As Their Numbers Rise, So Does Political Pull."

Gerrymandering for Position in 2002[1]

By Joshua Green
American Prospect, April 23, 2001

When Indiana Democrat Tim Roemer announced recently that he would retire from the House of Representatives at the end of this session of Congress, the officially cited reason was that he wanted to spend more time with his family. That's no doubt true. But it is surely also the case that Roemer didn't want to lose—as he most likely would have had he chosen to vie for re-election. Every 10 years, after the U.S. Census Bureau completes its tabulation of the country's inhabitants, congressional seats are reapportioned to reflect the state-by-state distribution of the population. Indiana's population has declined relative to other states' since 1990, so that when congressional lines are redrawn this year, the Hoosier State will lose a seat. Most experts predict that Roemer's South Bend district, which he carried last year by only 4 percent, will be expanded to include more conservative voters, making it much more difficult for the three-term Democrat to win re-election.

Roemer is the first congressman to bow out this session, but he won't be the last. Before the most recent round of redistricting in 1991, 65 House members chose to retire or seek another office. An additional 18 were forced to run against one another. With so many open seats and Congress so evenly divided, the stakes in this year's redistricting battle are higher than ever. In fact, control of Congress in 2002 could hinge on which party deals most deftly with redistricting—and on how state legislatures and the courts handle the disputes that will inevitably arise.

When congressional seats were reapportioned on December 28 to reflect the 2000 census, eight states in the South and West gained a total of 12 new seats while 10 northeastern and midwestern states (along with Oklahoma and Mississippi) lost a corresponding number. As a result, says Virginia representative Tom Davis, chairman of the National Republican Congressional Committee, "Republicans will pick up 10 to 14 seats, net, in the House." Noting that the states gaining seats tend to be conservative (and therefore likely to send new Republicans to Congress), and that the party holds many more

---

1. Reprinted with permission from *The American Prospect* Volume 12, Number 7: April 23, 2001. The American Prospect, 5 Broad Street, Boston, MA 02109. All rights reserved.

governorships and state legislatures (which is where most of the new congressional districts actually get redrawn) than it did 10 years ago, many Republicans insist that redistricting has made a GOP electoral bonanza inevitable.

It's not. It may even be that the population shift represents good news for Democrats: In six of the eight states adding seats, Hispanics—who voted two-to-one Democratic in the last election—accounted for most of the growth. "As far as winning back the House, [redistricting] means there are a whole lot more seats in play than there were two years ago," said one Democratic House strategist. "That's good for Democrats, especially going into a midterm election with a new Republican president." Nonpartisan experts tend to say it is too early to predict who will benefit from redistricting. "It's a wash in terms of where the votes are," said Mark Rush, a

---

"It's a wash in terms of where the votes are."—Mark Rush, Washington and Lee University

---

professor of politics at Washington and Lee University who studies redistricting. "It's not as if there is a reservoir of spare Republican voters looking to be farmed into the new congressional districts. There's still a Democratic majority out there."

It's true that Republicans are in a far better position than they were during the previous redistricting. In 1991 Republicans controlled both the governorship and the legislature in only two states, Utah and New Hampshire, which gave them effective oversight of only five congressional seats during redistricting. This year, in contrast, the GOP has possession of eight state legislatures, which—translated into congressional districts—gives Republicans effective control over 98 redistricted seats. Moreover, during the last decade Democrats have become more concentrated than ever in urban areas. This leaves them susceptible to political gerrymandering: Republicans can try to "pack" geographically concentrated Democrats into select congressional districts, leaving the surrounding districts more heavily conservative.

But the Republican gains since 1991 have brought them only to parity with the Democrats. In 2000 the electorate split the vote for the nation's 6,000 state candidates practically in half, leaving Republicans in control of eight state governments, Democrats in control of seven, and the two parties in divided control of the remaining 35. Translated into congressional seats subject to redistricting, this means that the Democrats control 101, the Republicans control 98, the two parties share control of 188, and independent commissions are in charge of 41 more. Judging by these numbers, redistricting will be as closely contested as the presidency.

A party's goal in redistricting is to draw boundaries that best serve its electoral interests. Both parties will try to emulate what Texas Democrats accomplished during the last round of redistricting—what one expert calls "the great partisan gerrymander of '91." The Democrats who controlled the legislature drew conservative districts around eight Republican incumbents. By packing conservatives into already heavily Republican districts, Democrats were able to win 21 of the 22 remaining seats.

Conversely, both parties will try to avoid the Georgia Democrats' debacle of that same year. Before redistricting, Georgia's 10-member delegation had just one Republican. But the Democrats were intent on redrawing his district to include more Democrats. Not only did they fail to oust the GOP incumbent (a guy by the name of Newt Gingrich); they overreached to the point that, today, eight of the state's 11 delegates are Republican. Democrats today attribute that outcome to carelessness. "Ten years ago, it never occurred to anyone that we might not be in the majority," said a Democratic strategist. "Now, the stakes are very high and very clear to all of us."

While neither party has a clear-cut advantage in the overall battle for seats, the fact that Republicans have drawn even with Democrats at the state level means that they'll have considerable opportunity to target veteran Democrats through redistricting. Among those considered most vulnerable are Lane Evans of Illinois, Sander Levin of Michigan, Martin Frost of Texas, and House Minority Whip David Bonior, who is contemplating a run for governor of Michigan.

Democrats stand to lose seats in states—such as Pennsylvania, Ohio, and Michigan—that are shedding congressional districts and are controlled by Republicans. They also face losses in states that have heavily Democratic delegations but only partial possession of state government, because split control makes partisan gerrymandering more difficult and tends to result in delegations that more accurately reflect the party composition of a state's electorate.

Democrats can expect to gain seats in states where they control the legislature—such as California, Georgia, Mississippi, and North Carolina. They'll also fare better in states with split control and heavily Republican delegations, like Georgia. And there is a good chance that Democrats can achieve partial victories in states such as Florida and Arizona. Florida's delegation currently consists of eight Democrats and 15 Republicans, with two new seats on the way. Because Florida's voters are split between the parties (as the 2000 election amply demonstrated), it will be nearly impossible for

Republican leaders to prevent at least one new seat from going Democratic and some of the existing Republican-held seats from becoming more competitive. The Arizona delegation, meanwhile, consists of five Republicans and a single Democrat. Even though the state has a Republican governor and legislature and is gaining two seats, a nonpartisan committee handles redistricting there and should draw the lines in a way that yields at least one more Democratic

> *The wild card in the redistricting battle will be the courts.*

seat—especially because with an influx of Hispanics and younger voters, Arizona is becoming more evenly split between the two parties. (In fact, because Arizona is one-third Hispanic but doesn't have a single Hispanic representative, a case could be made under the Voting Rights Act of 1965 that the group is being disenfranchised. The likely remedy would be the creation of a heavily Hispanic district in Phoenix or Tucson, which would presumably vote Democratic.)

The wild card in the redistricting battle will be the courts. Most of the states losing seats (Illinois, Mississippi, New York) have significant minority populations, while most of the states gaining seats (Arizona, California, Texas) attribute their growth to an increase in minorities. This is significant because the Voting Rights Act requires states with a history of discrimination against minority voters to use race as a factor when drawing congressional districts. In the past, courts have interpreted this to mean that a minority district must be drawn whenever possible to protect minority voting strength. To ensure that this standard is met, the Voting Rights Act requires all or parts of 16 states to "preclear" their redistricting maps with the Justice Department or the U.S. District Court in Washington, D.C.

But in 1993, in *Reno v. Shaw*, the Supreme Court determined that relying too heavily on race in drawing district lines violated the equal protection clause of the 14th Amendment. In 2000, in *Reno v. Bossier Parish School Board*, the Court reaffirmed that changes to minority districts could not lead to retrogression—but lowered the hurdle for getting preclearance, making it easier for states to draw districts that don't take into account minority voting strength and making it harder to create new minority districts. "The Supreme Court's decisions in this area have been very murky," said Gerry Hebert, general counsel for IMPAC 2000, the Democrats' national redistricting project. "But race is still going to be an important factor."

In truth, the new limit on race as a factor in redistricting may actually benefit Democrats. During the administration of Bush's father, the attorney general used the Voting Rights Act to justify allowing Republican-controlled states to pack minorities into a small number of districts, thereby diluting Democratic voting strength in surrounding areas. In calling for minority districts, the Republican Justice Department could cynically claim to be obeying the Voting Rights Act—when in fact it was doing the opposite. Now that the Court has limited the ability of states to take race into consideration, John Ashcroft's Justice Department will have a harder time employing this tactic.

With control of Congress hanging in the balance, the courts will undoubtedly have a larger role in redistricting than ever before. "Ten years ago, 41 states wound up in litigation," notes a Republican national redistricting expert. "A lot of attorneys out there would like to go 50 for 50 next year." Redistricting lawsuits are already under way in Texas, Utah, and North Carolina. And for the first time, the national parties will get involved in a process that is traditionally left to state lawmakers: The Democratic and Republican National Committees plan to devote millions of dollars to legal battles over redistricting.

The Supreme Court is divided over redistricting. Four justices—John Paul Stevens, David Souter, Ruth Bader Ginsburg, and Stephen Breyer—have made it clear that they oppose the Shaw doctrine's limitation on the use of race. The five justices in the majority tend to support the limitation, but for varying reasons. Justice Sandra Day O'Connor agrees with the liberal justices that race can be a principal factor, yet she also believes that in order to be constitutional the legislative response must be narrowly tailored; that is, districts can take race into account, but they must still be drawn compactly. The two most conservative jurists, Clarence Thomas and Antonin Scalia, oppose any consideration of race as a factor. (Ominously, the breakdown of justices mirrors *Bush v. Gore*.) The swing vote appears to lie, as so often happens, with O'Connor. Whichever way the Court decides, critical questions about redistricting are likely to be decided by a five-to-four vote.

In light of all this, neither party can afford to be confident about the effects of redistricting at this point. "They'll gain some seats, we'll gain some seats, and we'll end up pretty close," Hebert predicts. But an increasingly likely scenario is this one: Control of Congress could be decided like the presidential election—in court.

Connecticut Prepares to Sacrifice a Seat[2]

By Suzanne Dougherty
CQ Weekly, May 19, 2001

Connecticut is losing one of its six U.S. House seats as a result of the 2000 census. The state's political community now is gearing up for a bruising game of musical chairs, with the two parties holding sharply different ideas about how to fit six incumbents—Republicans Rob Simmons, Christopher Shays and Nancy L. Johnson and Democrats Jim Maloney, Rosa DeLauro and John B. Larson—into five districts.

Democrats argue that Simmons should be the odd man out. Simmons' upset victory in Connecticut's 2nd District was a highlight for the GOP in 2000: The 10-year state House member, regarded by both parties' strategists as the underdog in his challenge to 10-term Democratic Rep. Sam Gejdenson, closed strongly and scored a 51 percent to 49 percent win. But as the only freshman in the Connecticut delegation, he tops the Democrats' redistricting hit list.

Republicans, however, envision a different fall guy in redistricting: three-term Democrat Maloney of the 5th District. Maloney rather easily won a 2000 rematch with Republican Mark Nielsen after nearly losing to him in 1998. But his district is a mix of gritty urban and affluent suburban areas that Republicans contend could be readily annexed by neighboring districts; the elongated 5th is the only district that touches on all five others.

Initial responsibility for drawing the lines is held by an eight-member bipartisan committee: two Democrats and two Republicans each from the state House and Senate. If the committee is unable to produce a plan by its September 15 deadline, Republican Gov. John G. Rowland will appoint a commission made up of eight members—again four Republicans and four Democrats—who will appoint a ninth member to the panel. A new deadline of November 30 would take effect.

Should the committee meet the September 15 deadline, its plan would face a vote by the legislature. Although Democrats control both chambers by substantial margins—100 seats to the Republi-

---

cans' 51 in the state House, 21–15 in the Senate—that might not be enough to ensure passage of a Democratic-oriented plan: State law requires that a redistricting plan pass by two-thirds majorities in both chambers.

If the commission ends up being empaneled and meets its November 30 deadline, its re-map plan will have the force of law. Rowland has no veto power over redistricting and is relegated to a sideline role in the process.

> *The state had not lost a U.S. House seat since the 1840 census.*

The state Supreme Court will take control of the process if no plan is adopted by November 30. This has never happened in Connecticut, and the unpredictability of courts in other states' redistricting battles makes few politicians want to see it happen there.

Connecticut had long avoided the sort of redistricting chaos it faces this year. The state had not lost a U.S. House seat since the 1840 census. It has held at six seats since gaining one in the reapportionment following the 1930 census.

Yet this year's setback in Connecticut—which had a population increase of just 3.6 percent between 1990 and 2000—is typical of a decades-long trend that has seen population numbers and political clout shift from the historic industrial belt in the Northeast and Midwest to the South and West.

Eight of the 10 states that are losing House seats in the 2000 reapportionment are in the North and East. All eight states that are gaining seats are in the South and West.

Intrastate Shifts

Population growth rates over the past decade varied even among regions within Connecticut.

Suburban, mainly affluent Fairfield County near New York City—currently split between the 4th District represented by Republican Shays, Democrat Maloney's 5th District and the 6th District held by Republican Johnson—became the most populous county in the state.

The state's older jurisdictions moved in the other direction. The population in the state capital of Hartford, located in the 1st District and represented by Democrat Larson, declined by 15 percent between 1990 and 2000. New Haven, in Democrat DeLauro's 3rd District, and New London, in Simmons' 2nd District, were among the other cities that lost residents.

Because of reapportionment, all the state's current districts will undergo significant alteration—and one of them will disappear altogether.

It could be the 2nd, already the largest district geographically in the relatively compact state. The largely working-class eastern Connecticut district runs from the Long Island Sound waterfront in the south to the Massachusetts border in the north.

State Democrats favor splitting the 2nd District into two, with the towns along the eastern shoreline added to the 3rd District and the northern section added to the 1st District. Simmons would then be forced to run against either six-term Democrat DeLauro or two-term Democrat Larson, both of whom won re-election in 2000 with 72 percent of the vote.

Simmons' lack of seniority and the political clout that accompanies it place him at increased risk.

Maloney, who faces his own redistricting worries, appears eager to point the redistricting posse in Simmons' direction. "I think splitting up the 2nd makes sense in terms of population and fairness," said Maloney.

The 2nd has at least a modest Democratic lean: Democratic presidential nominee Al Gore (with Connecticut Sen. Joseph I. Lieberman as his vice presidential candidate) carried the 2nd in 2000 by 55 percent to 38 percent over George W. Bush, even as Simmons was upsetting longtime Democratic Rep. Gejdenson.

So Maloney concludes that dismantling the 2nd would not be a partisan attack, even if Simmons ended up losing his seat because of it.

"The 2nd is a Democratic district on paper, despite the fact that it is represented by a Republican. By splitting it up, we would be surrendering a Democratic district. No one really wins in that approach, which gives the plan a rough equity," Maloney said.

But eastern Connecticut officials, including Simmons, argue that this approach would be a disaster. They say eastern Connecticut, which is made up primarily of small towns and could be considered rural according to East Coast standards, has a unique set of issues and concerns that would be overshadowed if the region is merged with the mainly urban neighboring districts.

Simmons' potential plight has drawn the attention of House Republican leaders as they prepare to defend their narrow majority in the 2002 elections. House Speaker J. Dennis Hastert, R-Ill., visited New London on May 15 as the main attraction at a $500-per-person fundraiser for Simmons at the city's Radisson Hotel.

Taking the 5th?

Republicans, meanwhile, point to the 5th District's strategic location as a target for elimination in redistricting.

The 5th follows an irregular path from the state's western border to its mid-section, taking in the cities of Danbury and Waterbury. It includes cities and suburbs in Fairfield and New Haven counties.

Under the Republicans' concept, Waterbury and the towns in the 5th District's portion of New Haven County would be given to the 6th District. Danbury and some of the small Fairfield County suburbs would be added to the 4th District.

Republicans argue that this plan would cause the least disruption to other districts. They also say that dividing up the 5th is the fairest notion since it is the most politically competitive of the state's current districts.

The Democratic tendencies in Waterbury, Danbury and the city of Meriden are counterbalanced by two dozen smaller towns where Republican candidates usually run well among middle-class voters. There are two Fortune 500 companies in the district, whose offices employ a substantial white-collar work force.

The 5th has traits of a partisan "swing" district. It was represented by Republican Gary A. Franks (1991–97) for three terms until he was defeated in 1996 by Maloney (who had lost to Franks two years earlier). Maloney staved off GOP challenger Nielsen by just 50 percent to 48 percent in 1998, though he won their 2000 rematch by 54 percent to 44 percent.

Gore's 51 percent to 44 percent win over Bush in the 5th was his narrowest in any Connecticut district.

If the 5th were split up, Maloney would likely end up in 2002 facing one of two Republican moderates: Shays, reelected with 58 percent in the 4th District, or Johnson, who took 63 percent in her most recent 6th District race.

Though she generally has won her races easily, Johnson had a near-defeat experience in 1996, when she fended off Democrat Charlotte Koskoff by just 1,587 votes. Johnson already is expressing some concern about a possible redistricting-forced matchup with Maloney.

Johnson, chairman of the House Ways and Means Health Subcommittee, distributed literature at two March 20 Capitol Hill fundraisers urging her donors not to also give money to Maloney's campaign fund. "A campaign contribution for Jim Maloney is a contribution against Nancy Johnson," warned the notice.

The ultimate direction for Connecticut's redistricting process is likely to begin to take shape soon. The legislature's reapportionment committee has scheduled public hearings for late June and July in Bridgeport, New Haven, Waterbury, Hartford and Norwich.

Editor's note: The bipartisan Reapportionment Commision could not reach final agreement; therefore, on December 1, 2002, the entire matter was handed over to the Connecticut Supreme Court.

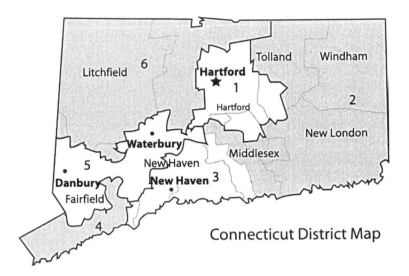

Connecticut District Map

Steady growth in the Connecticut suburbs of New York City helped the state maintain a six-seat House delegation for seven decades. But stagnant or declining population in the state's older cities finally caught up with Connecticut, which is losing one of its seats as a result of the 2000 census. The delegation is split between three Republicans (districts shaded in the map) and three Democrats, and all appear determined to seek re-election in 2002. Redistricting is to be initiated by an eight-member committee with equal numbers of Republicans and Democrats; if it approves a plan by Sept. 15, both chambers of the Democratic-controlled legislature would have to approve it by two-thirds votes. If that process failed, a nine-member bipartisan commission would take over, with a Nov. 30 deadline. Democrats want to split up the 2nd District, the only one represented by a freshman, Republican Rob Simmons. Republicans want to dismantle the 5th, held by Democrat Jim Maloney; this district touches on all five other districts.

Race to be the "Largest" Puts Minority Groups in Last Place[3]

BY JULIANNE MALVEAUX
BLACK ISSUES IN HIGHER EDUCATION, APRIL 12, 2001

The U.S. Census Bureau started releasing 2000 data in March. While demographic data is usually lackluster and mind-numbing, this time around headlines about population data resembles that which you would see for a horse race. "Census Figures Show Hispanics Pulling Even with Blacks," said the *New York Times*. "Latinos May Exceed Blacks in the U.S.," wrote the *Los Angeles Times*. The *Washington Post* said Hispanics had "drawn even" with Blacks, and the *Philadelphia Inquirer* described the two groups as being in a "virtual tie" for the dubious distinction of being the nation's largest minority group. Other words have been used to describe the relative size of the African American and Latino populations. African Americans have been, it is said, "outpaced," "overtaken" and "surpassed."

Did I miss something? When the last decennial data were collected, was there someone who said, "Ready, set, go, last one to reproduce at pace is a rotten egg?" Are African Americans and Hispanics in competition? For what? What does the fact that one group is larger than the other signify from a policy perspective? Both groups experience higher unemployment rates, lower incomes and more poverty than Whites. Both groups are underrepresented in the nation's corridors of power, from the seats of the U.S. Senate, to corporate board participation, to enrollment in our nation's elite law, business and medical schools. Neither group has its fair share of representation. Will the victor in the horse race be awarded the prize of fair treatment? I think not.

It is in the interest of many "colorblind" White Americans to set African Americans and Latinos at each other's throats. *Chicago Sun-Times* columnist George Will virtually salivated with glee on one of the Sunday morning chat shows, when he said the growing Latino population might put an end to the "racial spoils" system. He went on to say that the number of Hispanics and Asians combined,

---

"far outnumber African Americans." Should outnumbering African Americans become a goal of other populations of color, and if so, why?

> *Whether they coalesce or compete, each group has reasonable claims.*

If, despite growing populations of color, White folks insist on holding onto their slice of the pie, then African Americans, Latinos, Asians and American Indian people will squabble over "racial spoils." But if the allocation system is fair and reasonable, as minority population rises, so will their share of the pie. That means less for Whites. Thus, the conversation about racial competition.

Issues of African American entitlement won't go away, regardless of the growing Hispanic population. Those who feel that African Americans are entitled to reparations for slavery won't change their mind because the Hispanic population is growing. Those who say African Americans need to be better represented in our nation's schools and corporations won't change their position because of the increased size of the Hispanic population.

African Americans and Hispanics may choose to be complementary, not competitive, around issues of affirmative action and fair representation. But whether they coalesce or compete, each group has reasonable claims against a nation that, despite increasing diversity, retains remnants of racism.

Each population experiences racism differently, but relative size has little to do with the extent of the injury any group can claim. Less than 1 percent of our nation's population is American Indian, primarily because our country wiped out much of that population in a genocidal, territory-grabbing set of wars. If the Hispanic population were five times the size of the African American population, that would not minimize the barbarity of slavery and the inequality of its aftermath, nor would it change the appropriate remedy for that wrong.

In higher education, many have behaved as if they can focus on only one group of color at a time. Administrators shouldn't be asked to choose between providing services to African American or Latino students, not when both groups of students are underrepresented in the academy. Instead, both groups ought to be pushing for more services, more scholarships and better representation.

This push ought to extend to the public sector where the social service shuffle is, at best, saddening. I have heard Latino activists argue that African Americans discriminate against them in, say, the distribution of beds in a homeless shelter or spaces in a housing project. Is that what we now aspire to? Equality in poverty? Equal access for the homeless of color? I would like to think we could gather to eliminate our nation's homeless problem instead of squabbling over spaces in a shelter.

Don't get me wrong. There have been, and perhaps always will be, tensions between racial/ethnic groups in this country. But African Americans and Latinos have more in common than in contrast, especially around a set of educational and economic issues. Both groups will be losers if they let the arithmetic of White supremacy successfully divide and conquer.

As Their Numbers Rise, So Does Political Pull[4]

BY DANIEL B. WOOD
CHRISTIAN SCIENCE MONITOR, MARCH 16, 2001

The candidate for mayor of Los Angeles stepped up to the bank of microphones, ready to deliver his message about the plight of minority bus riders.

"Basic services are not available for people who need them the most," he says, squinting behind Ben Franklin eyeglasses. "As mayor, I will build a smarter, more efficient MTA."

More noteworthy than the press conference itself is the fact that candidate Xavier Becerra is competing in a mayoral field that includes not one, but two, Hispanics—and not a single African-American.

If the story of America is one in which rising minority groups eventually seize control of local political office, Los Angeles may well be its latest chapter. Although no politician with Mexican-American roots has been elected mayor here since 1870, L.A.'s expanding Latino population and rising Latino voter registration are expected to give Hispanic candidates in this spring's election their best showing in years.

Last week's report that Hispanics have officially replaced blacks as America's largest minority group may hold implications for political change far beyond Los Angeles. In some cases, Hispanics are expected to make gains in cities long dominated by white officeholders. In multi-ethnic cities such as Los Angeles, they may fight for seats held by other minorities.

"The Los Angeles mayoral race is but one local manifestation of a national demographic change that we have long known is coming but is now here," says Silvia Puentes of the Institute for Latino Studies at Notre Dame University in South Bend, Ind. "The idea of this country as fundamentally a black-versus-white paradigm is now officially outmoded."

---

4. This article first appeared in *The Christian Science Monitor* on March 16, 2001, and is reproduced with permission. Copyright © 2001 The Christian Science Monitor. All rights reserved. Online at *csmonitor.com*.

How this demographic reality plays out in terms of political power will depend in part on where the new Hispanic growth is concentrated. That information is coming out from new 2000 census reports in dribs and drabs, and is still preliminary.

In recent decades, Hispanics have lived primarily in California, Arizona, Texas, New Mexico, Florida, Colorado, Illinois, Massachusetts, and Nevada. If the new numbers are added to those states, say observers, Hispanics are likely to increase their representation in Congress. And their influence on the highest state and federal offices—such as senator, governor, and presidential candidates—will also be greater.

Here in California, those advances are already coming. Hispanics now claim about one-third of the seats in the state legislature, as well as the high-powered posts of lieutenant governor and, until recently, Assembly Speaker.

Some observers say the rise of Hispanics is leading to a new era of coalition-building . . . others, however, see competition at every level.

But the political impact of America's newly counted 35.3 million Hispanics is likely to be felt most strongly in cities and towns. And that's where tensions between the nation's two largest minority groups have occasionally flared.

In Watts, a gritty Los Angeles neighborhood once populated mostly by blacks, Hispanics now make up 60 percent of the residents.

"Even though Latinos outnumber blacks in the population, blacks maintain power from the city council to the school board," says Najee Ali, a black minister from South Central, which includes Watts.

Some observers say the rise of Hispanics is leading to a new era of coalition-building between two minority groups that realize they must stick together to achieve mutual aims.

Others, however, see competition at every level. Many Hispanics in California felt they did not get enough support in fighting Proposition 187, a 1994 ballot initiative to curb services such as education to illegal immigrants. Meanwhile, many blacks felt they did not get enough support on Proposition 209, ending affirmative action at state colleges and in state hiring and contracting.

"There has been tension between these two races on political representation, as well as the fight for jobs," says Mr. Ali. "This is reflected by tension in the schools between kids, and between adults fighting for jobs. Many blacks supporting large families have been displaced by Latinos willing to work for less wages."

But Ali and others say much of the resistance is generational, that older blacks accustomed to a more dominant position are less able to embrace Hispanics. Younger members of both groups, he says, find it easier to move ahead together.

> *"The point is, how will the change be addressed— as threat or opportunity?"*—Mark Ridley Thomas, city councilor, South Central Los Angeles

"We are very young," says Juan Salgado, director of the Chicago-based Institute for Latino Progress, noting that in big cities with large numbers of Hispanics, more than half the Latino population is younger than 21. "That means we are not carrying a lot of racial or social baggage and are open to making things work," he says.

Before Hispanics can come into their own, however, their voter-registration rates will need to improve. Although they now make up about 13 percent of the U.S. population, according to preliminary U.S. Census Bureau figures, they are only about 5 percent of voters.

"These newly released figures should be a wake-up call both for middle Americans and Easterners who have been ignoring us for the past 20 years," says Antonio Gonzalez, executive director of the Southwest Voter Registration and Education Project. "But it is also a wake-up for Hispanics who have suffered because they are not as politically active as their numbers might suggest."

That is reflected nationally in the statistic that the Congressional Black Caucus is still roughly twice the size of the Congressional Hispanic Caucus.

While many look at such numbers and see trouble and competitiveness ahead for blacks and Hispanics, others see only changing times.

"This by no means ought to be seen as a negative," says Mark Ridley Thomas, a black city councilor representing part of South Central Los Angeles. "The point is, how will the change be addressed— as threat or opportunity? No group is more experienced in coalition-building than African-Americans. We feel this is a time to tap into that experience."

Editor's note: James K. Hahn won the mayoral election, with the support of both African Americans and conservative whites. Rocky Delgadillo won the post of city attorney, becoming the first Latino to be elected to citywide office in modern-day Los Angeles.

Appendix

The Long Form, 2000

PLEASE DO NOT FILL OUT THIS FORM.
This is not an official census form. It is for informational purposes only.

United States
Census 2000

U.S. Department of Commerce
Bureau of the Census

This is the official form for all the people at this address. It is quick and easy, and your answers are protected by law. Complete the Census and help your community get what it needs — today and in the future!

The "Informational Copy" shows the content of the United States Census 2000 "long" form questionnaire. Each household will receive either a short form (100-percent questions) or a long form (100-percent and sample questions). The long form questionnaire includes the same 6 population questions and 1 housing question that are on the Census 2000 short form, plus 26 additional population questions, and 20 additional housing questions. On average, about 1 in every 6 households will receive the long form. The content of the forms resulted from reviewing the 1990 census data, consulting with federal and non-federal data users, and conducting tests.

For additional information about Census 2000, visit our website at **www.census.gov** or write to the Director, Bureau of the Census, Washington, DC 20233.

Start Here
Please use a black or blue pen.

1 How many people were living or staying in this house, apartment, or mobile home on April 1, 2000?

Number of people

INCLUDE in this number:
- foster children, roomers, or housemates
- people staying here on April 1, 2000 who have no other permanent place to stay
- people living here most of the time while working, even if they have another place to live

DO NOT INCLUDE in this number:
- college students living away while attending college
- people in a correctional facility, nursing home, or mental hospital on April 1, 2000
- Armed Forces personnel living somewhere else
- people who live or stay at another place most of the time

➡ Please turn the page and print the names of all the people living or staying here on April 1, 2000.

If you need help completing this form, *call 1–800–XXX–XXXX between 8:00 a.m. and 9:00 p.m., 7 days a week. The telephone call is free.*
TDD – *Telephone display device for the hearing impaired. Call 1–800–XXX–XXXX between 8:00 a.m. and 9:00 p.m., 7 days a week. The telephone call is free.*
¿NECESITA AYUDA? *Si usted necesita ayuda para completar este cuestionario llame al 1–800–XXX–XXXX entre las 8:00 a.m. y las 9:00 p.m., 7 días a la semana. La llamada telefónica es gratis.*

The Census Bureau estimates that, for the average household, this form will take about 38 minutes to complete, including the time for reviewing the instructions and answers. Comments about the estimate should be directed to the Associate Director for Finance and Administration, Attn: Paperwork Reduction Project 0607-0856, Room 3104, Federal Building 3, Bureau of the Census, Washington, DC 20233.
Respondents are not required to respond to any information collection unless it displays a valid approval number from the Office of Management and Budget.

Form **D-61B**

OMB No. 0607-0856: Approval Expires 12/31/2000

List of Persons

➡ **Please be sure you answered question 1 on the front page before continuing.**

② **Please print the names of all the people who you indicated in question 1 were living or staying here on April 1, 2000.**
Example — Last Name

J O H N S O N

First Name   MI

R O B I N   *J*

Start with the person, or one of the people living here who owns, is buying, or rents this house, apartment, or mobile home. If there is no such person, start with any adult living or staying here.

Person 1 — Last Name

First Name   MI

Person 2 — Last Name

First Name   MI

Person 3 — Last Name

First Name   MI

Person 4 — Last Name

First Name   MI

Person 5 — Last Name

First Name   MI

Person 6 — Last Name

First Name   MI

Person 7 — Last Name

First Name   MI

Person 8 — Last Name

First Name   MI

Person 9 — Last Name

First Name   MI

Person 10 — Last Name

First Name   MI

Person 11 — Last Name

First Name   MI

Person 12 — Last Name

First Name   MI

➡ **Next, answer questions about Person 1.**

FOR OFFICE USE ONLY			
A. JIC1	**B. JIC2**	**C. JIC3**	**D. JIC4**

Form D-61B

2

Person 1

Your answers are important! Every person in the Census counts.

☞ **1** **What is this person's name?** *Print the name of Person 1 from page 2.*

Last Name

First Name   MI

2 **What is this person's telephone number?** *We may contact this person if we don't understand an answer.*

Area Code + Number

☞ **3** **What is this person's sex?** *Mark ☒ ONE box.*
- ☐ Male
- ☐ Female

☞ **4** **What is this person's age and what is this person's date of birth?**

Age on April 1, 2000

Print numbers in boxes.
Month   Day   Year of birth

➡ **NOTE: Please answer BOTH Questions 5 and 6.**

☞ **5** **Is this person Spanish/Hispanic/Latino?** *Mark ☒ the "No" box if not Spanish/Hispanic/Latino.*
- ☐ **No**, not Spanish/Hispanic/Latino
- ☐ Yes, Mexican, Mexican Am., Chicano
- ☐ Yes, Puerto Rican
- ☐ Yes, Cuban
- ☐ Yes, other Spanish/Hispanic/Latino — *Print group.* ↘

☞ **6** **What is this person's race?** *Mark ☒ one or more races to indicate what this person considers himself/herself to be.*
- ☐ White
- ☐ Black, African Am., or Negro
- ☐ American Indian or Alaska Native — *Print name of enrolled or principal tribe.* ↘

- ☐ Asian Indian
- ☐ Chinese
- ☐ Filipino
- ☐ Japanese
- ☐ Korean
- ☐ Vietnamese
- ☐ Other Asian — *Print race.* ↘

- ☐ Native Hawaiian
- ☐ Guamanian or Chamorro
- ☐ Samoan
- ☐ Other Pacific Islander — *Print race.* ↗

- ☐ Some other race — *Print race.* ↘

7 **What is this person's marital status?**
- ☐ Now married
- ☐ Widowed
- ☐ Divorced
- ☐ Separated
- ☐ Never married

8 **a. At any time since February 1, 2000, has this person attended regular school or college?** *Include only nursery school or preschool, kindergarten, elementary school, and schooling which leads to a high school diploma or a college degree.*
- ☐ No, has not attended since February 1 → *Skip to 9*
- ☐ Yes, public school, public college
- ☐ Yes, private school, private college

☞ Question is asked of all persons on the short (100-percent) and long (sample) forms.

Person 1 (continued)

8 **b. What grade or level was this person attending?** *Mark ☒ ONE box.*

- ☐ Nursery school, preschool
- ☐ Kindergarten
- ☐ Grade 1 to grade 4
- ☐ Grade 5 to grade 8
- ☐ Grade 9 to grade 12
- ☐ College undergraduate years (freshman to senior)
- ☐ Graduate or professional school *(for example: medical, dental, or law school)*

9 **What is the highest degree or level of school this person has COMPLETED?** *Mark ☒ ONE box.* *If currently enrolled, mark the previous grade or highest degree received.*

- ☐ No schooling completed
- ☐ Nursery school to 4th grade
- ☐ 5th grade or 6th grade
- ☐ 7th grade or 8th grade
- ☐ 9th grade
- ☐ 10th grade
- ☐ 11th grade
- ☐ 12th grade, **NO DIPLOMA**
- ☐ **HIGH SCHOOL GRADUATE** — high school DIPLOMA or the equivalent *(for example: GED)*
- ☐ Some college credit, but less than 1 year
- ☐ 1 or more years of college, no degree
- ☐ Associate degree *(for example: AA, AS)*
- ☐ Bachelor's degree *(for example: BA, AB, BS)*
- ☐ Master's degree *(for example: MA, MS, MEng, MEd, MSW, MBA)*
- ☐ Professional degree *(for example: MD, DDS, DVM, LLB, JD)*
- ☐ Doctorate degree *(for example: PhD, EdD)*

10 **What is this person's ancestry or ethnic origin?**

(For example: Italian, Jamaican, African Am., Cambodian, Cape Verdean, Norwegian, Dominican, French Canadian, Haitian, Korean, Lebanese, Polish, Nigerian, Mexican, Taiwanese, Ukrainian, and so on.)

11 **a. Does this person speak a language other than English at home?**

- ☐ Yes
- ☐ No → *Skip to 12*

b. What is this language?

(For example: Korean, Italian, Spanish, Vietnamese)

c. How well does this person speak English?

- ☐ Very well
- ☐ Well
- ☐ Not well
- ☐ Not at all

12 **Where was this person born?**

- ☐ In the United States — *Print name of state.*

- ☐ Outside the United States — *Print name of foreign country, or Puerto Rico, Guam, etc.*

13 **Is this person a CITIZEN of the United States?**

- ☐ Yes, born in the United States → *Skip to 15a*
- ☐ Yes, born in Puerto Rico, Guam, the U.S. Virgin Islands, or Northern Marianas
- ☐ Yes, born abroad of American parent or parents
- ☐ Yes, a U.S. citizen by naturalization
- ☐ No, not a citizen of the United States

14 **When did this person come to live in the United States?** *Print numbers in boxes.*

Year

15 **a. Did this person live in this house or apartment 5 years ago (on April 1, 1995)?**

- ☐ Person is under 5 years old → *Skip to 33*
- ☐ Yes, this house → *Skip to 16*
- ☐ No, outside the United States — *Print name of foreign country, or Puerto Rico, Guam, etc., below; then skip to 16.*

- ☐ No, different house in the United States

Person 1 (continued)

15 **b. Where did this person live 5 years ago?**

Name of city, town, or post office

Did this person live inside the limits of the city or town?

☐ Yes
☐ No, outside the city/town limits

Name of county

Name of state

ZIP Code

16 **Does this person have any of the following long-lasting conditions:**

	Yes	No
a. Blindness, deafness, or a severe vision or hearing impairment?	☐	☐
b. A condition that substantially limits one or more basic physical activities such as walking, climbing stairs, reaching, lifting, or carrying?	☐	☐

17 **Because of a physical, mental, or emotional condition lasting 6 months or more, does this person have any difficulty in doing any of the following activities:**

	Yes	No
a. Learning, remembering, or concentrating?	☐	☐
b. Dressing, bathing, or getting around inside the home?	☐	☐
c. (Answer if this person is 16 YEARS OLD OR OVER.) Going outside the home alone to shop or visit a doctor's office?	☐	☐
d. (Answer if this person is 16 YEARS OLD OR OVER.) Working at a job or business?	☐	☐

18 **Was this person under 15 years of age on April 1, 2000?**

☐ Yes → *Skip to 33*
☐ No

19 **a. Does this person have any of his/her own grandchildren under the age of 18 living in this house or apartment?**

☐ Yes
☐ No → *Skip to 20a*

b. Is this grandparent currently responsible for most of the basic needs of any grandchild(ren) under the age of 18 who live(s) in this house or apartment?

☐ Yes
☐ No → *Skip to 20a*

c. How long has this grandparent been responsible for the(se) grandchild(ren)? *If the grandparent is financially responsible for more than one grandchild, answer the question for the grandchild for whom the grandparent has been responsible for the longest period of time.*

☐ Less than 6 months
☐ 6 to 11 months
☐ 1 or 2 years
☐ 3 or 4 years
☐ 5 years or more

20 **a. Has this person ever served on active duty in the U.S. Armed Forces, military Reserves, or National Guard?** *Active duty does not include training for the Reserves or National Guard, but DOES include activation, for example, for the Persian Gulf War.*

☐ Yes, now on active duty
☐ Yes, on active duty in past, but not now
☐ No, training for Reserves or National Guard only → *Skip to 21*
☐ No, never served in the military → *Skip to 21*

b. When did this person serve on active duty in the U.S. Armed Forces? *Mark ☒ a box for EACH period in which this person served.*

☐ April 1995 or later
☐ August 1990 to March 1995 (including Persian Gulf War)
☐ September 1980 to July 1990
☐ May 1975 to August 1980
☐ Vietnam era (August 1964—April 1975)
☐ February 1955 to July 1964
☐ Korean conflict (June 1950—January 1955)
☐ World War II (September 1940—July 1947)
☐ Some other time

c. In total, how many years of active-duty military service has this person had?

☐ Less than 2 years
☐ 2 years or more

2045

Form D-61B

5

Person 1 (continued)

21 **LAST WEEK, did this person do ANY work for either pay or profit?** *Mark ☒ the "Yes" box even if the person worked only 1 hour, or helped without pay in a family business or farm for 15 hours or more, or was on active duty in the Armed Forces.*

☐ Yes
☐ No → *Skip to 25a*

22 **At what location did this person work LAST WEEK?** *If this person worked at more than one location, print where he or she worked most last week.*

a. Address (Number and street name)

(If the exact address is not known, give a description of the location such as the building name or the nearest street or intersection.)

b. Name of city, town, or post office

c. Is the work location inside the limits of that city or town?

☐ Yes
☐ No, outside the city/town limits

d. Name of county

e. Name of U.S. state or foreign country

f. ZIP Code

23 **a. How did this person usually get to work LAST WEEK?** *If this person usually used more than one method of transportation during the trip, mark ☒ the box of the one used for most of the distance.*

☐ Car, truck, or van
☐ Bus or trolley bus
☐ Streetcar or trolley car
☐ Subway or elevated
☐ Railroad
☐ Ferryboat
☐ Taxicab
☐ Motorcycle
☐ Bicycle
☐ Walked
☐ Worked at home → *Skip to 27*
☐ Other method

→ If "Car, truck, or van" is marked in 23a, go to 23b. Otherwise, skip to 24a.

23 **b. How many people, including this person, usually rode to work in the car, truck, or van LAST WEEK?**

☐ Drove alone
☐ 2 people
☐ 3 people
☐ 4 people
☐ 5 or 6 people
☐ 7 or more people

24 **a. What time did this person usually leave home to go to work LAST WEEK?**

☐ a.m. ☐ p.m.

b. How many minutes did it usually take this person to get from home to work LAST WEEK?

Minutes

⟳ Answer questions 25–26 for persons who did not work for pay or profit last week. Others skip to 27.

25 **a. LAST WEEK, was this person on layoff from a job?**

☐ Yes → *Skip to 25c*
☐ No

b. LAST WEEK, was this person TEMPORARILY absent from a job or business?

☐ Yes, on vacation, temporary illness, labor dispute, etc. → *Skip to 26*
☐ No → *Skip to 25d*

c. Has this person been informed that he or she will be recalled to work within the next 6 months OR been given a date to return to work?

☐ Yes → *Skip to 25e*
☐ No

d. Has this person been looking for work during the last 4 weeks?

☐ Yes
☐ No → *Skip to 26*

e. LAST WEEK, could this person have started a job if offered one, or returned to work if recalled?

☐ Yes, could have gone to work
☐ No, because of own temporary illness
☐ No, because of all other reasons *(in school, etc.)*

26 **When did this person last work, even for a few days?**

☐ 1995 to 2000
☐ 1994 or earlier, or never worked → *Skip to 31*

Form D-61B

Person 1 (continued)

27 **Industry or Employer** — *Describe clearly this person's chief job activity or business last week. If this person had more than one job, describe the one at which this person worked the most hours. If this person had no job or business last week, give the information for his/her last job or business since 1995.*

a. For whom did this person work? *If now on active duty in the Armed Forces, mark* ☒ *this box* → ☐ *and print the branch of the Armed Forces.*

Name of company, business, or other employer

b. What kind of business or industry was this? *Describe the activity at location where employed. (For example: hospital, newspaper publishing, mail order house, auto repair shop, bank)*

c. Is this mainly — *Mark* ☒ *ONE box.*
☐ Manufacturing?
☐ Wholesale trade?
☐ Retail trade?
☐ Other *(agriculture, construction, service, government, etc.)?*

28 **Occupation**
a. What kind of work was this person doing? *(For example: registered nurse, personnel manager, supervisor of order department, auto mechanic, accountant)*

b. What were this person's most important activities or duties? *(For example: patient care, directing hiring policies, supervising order clerks, repairing automobiles, reconciling financial records)*

29 **Was this person** — *Mark* ☒ *ONE box.*
☐ Employee of a PRIVATE-FOR-PROFIT company or business or of an individual, for wages, salary, or commissions
☐ Employee of a PRIVATE NOT-FOR-PROFIT, tax-exempt, or charitable organization
☐ Local GOVERNMENT employee *(city, county, etc.)*
☐ State GOVERNMENT employee
☐ Federal GOVERNMENT employee
☐ SELF-EMPLOYED in own NOT INCORPORATED business, professional practice, or farm
☐ SELF-EMPLOYED in own INCORPORATED business, professional practice, or farm
☐ Working WITHOUT PAY in family business or farm

30 **a. LAST YEAR, 1999, did this person work at a job or business at any time?**
☐ Yes
☐ No → *Skip to 31*

b. How many weeks did this person work in 1999? *Count paid vacation, paid sick leave, and military service.*
Weeks

c. During the weeks WORKED in 1999, how many hours did this person usually work each WEEK?
Usual hours worked each WEEK

31 **INCOME IN 1999** — *Mark* ☒ *the "Yes" box for each income source received during 1999 and enter the total amount received during 1999 to a maximum of $999,999. Mark* ☒ *the "No" box if the income source was not received. If net income was a loss, enter the amount and mark* ☒ *the "Loss" box next to the dollar amount.*

For income received jointly, report, if possible, the appropriate share for each person; otherwise, report the whole amount for only one person and mark ☒ *the "No" box for the other person. If exact amount is not known, please give best estimate.*

a. Wages, salary, commissions, bonuses, or tips from all jobs — *Report amount before deductions for taxes, bonds, dues, or other items.*
☐ Yes   Annual amount — *Dollars*
$ _ _ _ _ _ .00
☐ No

b. Self-employment income from own nonfarm businesses or farm businesses, including proprietorships and partnerships — *Report NET income after business expenses.*
☐ Yes   Annual amount — *Dollars*
$ _ _ _ _ _ .00   ☐ Loss
☐ No

2047

Form D-61B

7

Person 1 (continued)

31 c. Interest, dividends, net rental income, royalty income, or income from estates and trusts — *Report even small amounts credited to an account.*

☐ Yes   Annual amount — *Dollars*

$ ☐ Loss

☐ No

d. Social Security or Railroad Retirement

☐ Yes   Annual amount — *Dollars*

$

☐ No

e. Supplemental Security Income (SSI)

☐ Yes   Annual amount — *Dollars*

$

☐ No

f. Any public assistance or welfare payments from the state or local welfare office

☐ Yes   Annual amount — *Dollars*

$

☐ No

g. Retirement, survivor, or disability pensions — *Do NOT include Social Security.*

☐ Yes   Annual amount — *Dollars*

$

☐ No

h. Any other sources of income received regularly such as Veterans' (VA) payments, unemployment compensation, child support, or alimony — *Do NOT include lump-sum payments such as money from an inheritance or sale of a home.*

☐ Yes   Annual amount — *Dollars*

$

☐ No

32 What was this person's total income in 1999? *Add entries in questions 31a—31h; subtract any losses. If net income was a loss, enter the amount and mark ☒ the "Loss" box next to the dollar amount.*

Annual amount — *Dollars*

☐ None   OR $ ☐ Loss

☞ Question is asked of all households on the short (100-percent) and long (sample) forms.

HOUSING QUESTIONS

→ **Now, please answer questions 33—53 about your household.**

☞ **33 Is this house, apartment, or mobile home —**

☐ Owned by you or someone in this household with a mortgage or loan?
☐ Owned by you or someone in this household free and clear (without a mortgage or loan)?
☐ Rented for cash rent?
☐ Occupied without payment of cash rent?

34 Which best describes this building? *Include all apartments, flats, etc., even if vacant.*

☐ A mobile home
☐ A one-family house detached from any other house
☐ A one-family house attached to one or more houses
☐ A building with 2 apartments
☐ A building with 3 or 4 apartments
☐ A building with 5 to 9 apartments
☐ A building with 10 to 19 apartments
☐ A building with 20 to 49 apartments
☐ A building with 50 or more apartments
☐ Boat, RV, van, etc.

35 About when was this building first built?

☐ 1999 or 2000
☐ 1995 to 1998
☐ 1990 to 1994
☐ 1980 to 1989
☐ 1970 to 1979
☐ 1960 to 1969
☐ 1950 to 1959
☐ 1940 to 1949
☐ 1939 or earlier

36 When did this person move into this house, apartment, or mobile home?

☐ 1999 or 2000
☐ 1995 to 1998
☐ 1990 to 1994
☐ 1980 to 1989
☐ 1970 to 1979
☐ 1969 or earlier

37 How many rooms do you have in this house, apartment, or mobile home? *Do NOT count bathrooms, porches, balconies, foyers, halls, or half-rooms.*

☐ 1 room   ☐ 6 rooms
☐ 2 rooms   ☐ 7 rooms
☐ 3 rooms   ☐ 8 rooms
☐ 4 rooms   ☐ 9 or more rooms
☐ 5 rooms

Person 1 (continued)

38 How many bedrooms do you have; that is, how many bedrooms would you list if this house, apartment, or mobile home were on the market for sale or rent?

☐ No bedroom
☐ 1 bedroom
☐ 2 bedrooms
☐ 3 bedrooms
☐ 4 bedrooms
☐ 5 or more bedrooms

39 Do you have COMPLETE plumbing facilities in this house, apartment, or mobile home; that is, 1) hot and cold piped water, 2) a flush toilet, and 3) a bathtub or shower?

☐ Yes, have all three facilities
☐ No

40 Do you have COMPLETE kitchen facilities in this house, apartment, or mobile home; that is, 1) a sink with piped water, 2) a range or stove, and 3) a refrigerator?

☐ Yes, have all three facilities
☐ No

41 Is there telephone service available in this house, apartment, or mobile home from which you can both make and receive calls?

☐ Yes
☐ No

42 Which FUEL is used MOST for heating this house, apartment, or mobile home?

☐ Gas: from underground pipes serving the neighborhood
☐ Gas: bottled, tank, or LP
☐ Electricity
☐ Fuel oil, kerosene, etc.
☐ Coal or coke
☐ Wood
☐ Solar energy
☐ Other fuel
☐ No fuel used

43 How many automobiles, vans, and trucks of one-ton capacity or less are kept at home for use by members of your household?

☐ None
☐ 1
☐ 2
☐ 3
☐ 4
☐ 5
☐ 6 or more

44 Answer ONLY if this is a ONE-FAMILY HOUSE OR MOBILE HOME — All others skip to 45.

a. Is there a business (such as a store or barber shop) or a medical office on this property?

☐ Yes
☐ No

b. How many acres is this house or mobile home on?

☐ Less than 1 acre → *Skip to 45*
☐ 1 to 9.9 acres
☐ 10 or more acres

c. In 1999, what were the actual sales of all agricultural products from this property?

☐ None
☐ $1 to $999
☐ $1,000 to $2,499
☐ $2,500 to $4,999
☐ $5,000 to $9,999
☐ $10,000 or more

45 What are the annual costs of utilities and fuels for this house, apartment, or mobile home? *If you have lived here less than 1 year, estimate the annual cost.*

a. Electricity

Annual cost — *Dollars*

$ ___ , ___ ___ ___ .00

OR

☐ Included in rent or in condominium fee
☐ No charge or electricity not used

b. Gas

Annual cost — *Dollars*

$ ___ , ___ ___ ___ .00

OR

☐ Included in rent or in condominium fee
☐ No charge or gas not used

c. Water and sewer

Annual cost — *Dollars*

$ ___ , ___ ___ ___ .00

OR

☐ Included in rent or in condominium fee
☐ No charge

d. Oil, coal, kerosene, wood, etc.

Annual cost — *Dollars*

$ ___ , ___ ___ ___ .00

OR

☐ Included in rent or in condominium fee
☐ No charge or these fuels not used

2049

Form D-61B

9

Person 1 (continued)

46 Answer ONLY if you PAY RENT for this house, apartment, or mobile home — All others skip to 47.

a. What is the monthly rent?

Monthly amount — *Dollars*

$ ⬚ ⬚ ⬚ .00

b. Does the monthly rent include any meals?

☐ Yes
☐ No

47 Answer questions 47a—53 if you or someone in this household owns or is buying this house, apartment, or mobile home; otherwise, skip to questions for Person 2.

a. Do you have a mortgage, deed of trust, contract to purchase, or similar debt on THIS property?

☐ Yes, mortgage, deed of trust, or similar debt
☐ Yes, contract to purchase
☐ No → *Skip to 48a*

b. How much is your regular monthly mortgage payment on THIS property? *Include payment only on first mortgage or contract to purchase.*

Monthly amount — *Dollars*

$ ⬚ ⬚ ⬚ .00

OR

☐ No regular payment required → *Skip to 48a*

c. Does your regular monthly mortgage payment include payments for real estate taxes on THIS property?

☐ Yes, taxes included in mortgage payment
☐ No, taxes paid separately or taxes not required

d. Does your regular monthly mortgage payment include payments for fire, hazard, or flood insurance on THIS property?

☐ Yes, insurance included in mortgage payment
☐ No, insurance paid separately or no insurance

48 a. Do you have a second mortgage or a home equity loan on THIS property? *Mark ⌧ all boxes that apply.*

☐ Yes, a second mortgage
☐ Yes, a home equity loan
☐ No → *Skip to 49*

b. How much is your regular monthly payment on all second or junior mortgages and all home equity loans on THIS property?

Monthly amount — *Dollars*

$ ⬚ ⬚ ⬚ .00

OR

☐ No regular payment required

49 What were the real estate taxes on THIS property last year?

Yearly amount — *Dollars*

$ ⬚ ⬚ ⬚ .00

OR

☐ None

50 What was the annual payment for fire, hazard, and flood insurance on THIS property?

Annual amount — *Dollars*

$ ⬚ ⬚ ⬚ .00

OR

☐ None

51 What is the value of this property; that is, how much do you think this house and lot, apartment, or mobile home and lot would sell for if it were for sale?

☐ Less than $10,000
☐ $10,000 to $14,999
☐ $15,000 to $19,999
☐ $20,000 to $24,999
☐ $25,000 to $29,999
☐ $30,000 to $34,999
☐ $35,000 to $39,999
☐ $40,000 to $49,999
☐ $50,000 to $59,999
☐ $60,000 to $69,999
☐ $70,000 to $79,999
☐ $80,000 to $89,999
☐ $90,000 to $99,999
☐ $100,000 to $124,999
☐ $125,000 to $149,999
☐ $150,000 to $174,999
☐ $175,000 to $199,999
☐ $200,000 to $249,999
☐ $250,000 to $299,999
☐ $300,000 to $399,999
☐ $400,000 to $499,999
☐ $500,000 to $749,999
☐ $750,000 to $999,999
☐ $1,000,000 or more

52 Answer ONLY if this is a CONDOMINIUM —

What is the monthly condominium fee?

Monthly amount — *Dollars*

$ ⬚ ⬚ ⬚ .00

53 Answer ONLY if this is a MOBILE HOME —

a. Do you have an installment loan or contract on THIS mobile home?

☐ Yes
☐ No

b. What was the total cost for installment loan payments, personal property taxes, site rent, registration fees, and license fees on THIS mobile home and its site last year? *Exclude real estate taxes.*

Yearly amount — *Dollars*

$ ⬚ ⬚ ⬚ .00

➡ **Are there more people living here? If yes, continue with Person 2.**

Person 2

Census information helps your community get financial assistance for roads, hospitals, schools and more.

1 **What is this person's name?** *Print the name of Person 2 from page 2.*

Last Name

First Name   MI

☞ **2** **How is this person related to Person 1?**
Mark ☒ ONE box.

☐ Husband/wife
☐ Natural-born son/daughter
☐ Adopted son/daughter
☐ Stepson/stepdaughter
☐ Brother/sister
☐ Father/mother
☐ Grandchild
☐ Parent-in-law
☐ Son-in-law/daughter-in-law
☐ Other relative — *Print exact relationship.*

If NOT RELATED to Person 1:

☐ Roomer, boarder
☐ Housemate, roommate
☐ Unmarried partner
☐ Foster child
☐ Other nonrelative

☞ Question is asked of Persons 2–6 on the short (100-percent) and long (sample) forms.

For Person 2, repeat questions 3-32 of Person 1.

2051

Form D-61B

11

Person

3

Information about
children helps your
community plan for
child care, education,
and recreation.

For Persons 3–6. repeat questions 1-32 of Person 2.

NOTE – *The content for Question 2 varies between Person 1 and Persons 2–6.*

Thank you for completing your official U.S. Census form. If there are more than six people at this address, the Census Bureau may contact you for the same information about these people.

Census-taker's Form, 1900

In the census of 1900, the records were compiled by census-takers called enumerators, who visited every dwelling place, questioned the inhabitants, and added their names to the form that is reproduced (and then enlarged) below. There were pages of instructions for the enumerator, who was advised to ask the same question two different ways when the answer seemed doubtful, to interview neighbors if the person was always out, and to distinguish occupations carefully--a housewife was not to be listed as a housekeeper, who could only be a paid employee, and "worker in a carriage factory" was unacceptably vague, for there were half a dozen specialized crafts involved in building a horse-drawn carriage. As the form shows, children who survived infancy might be at work by age 10. The questions on education would now be considered minimal.

TWELFTH CENSUS OF THE UNITED STATES

SCHEDULE No. 1—POPULATION

State _ _ _ _ _ _ }
County _ _ _ _ _ _
Township or other division of county _ _ _ _ _ _

Name of incorporated city, town, or village within the above-named division, _ _ _ _ _ _

Enumerated by me on the _ _ _ day of June, 1900, _ _ _ _ _ _, Enumerator.

Supervisor's District No. _ _ _ _ _ }
Enumeration District No. _ _ _ _ _ }

Sheet No. _ _ _

Ward of city, _ _ _ _ _ _

Census-taker's Form, 1900, enlarged section (a)

State ----------------- }

County ----------------

Township or other division of county ----------- [Insert name

Name of incorporated city, town, or village within the Enumerated by

LOCATION.				NAME	RELATION.
IN CITIES		Number of dwelling, house in the order of visitation.	Number of family, in the order of visitation	of each person whose place of abode on June 1, 1900, was in this family Enter surname first, then the given name and middle initial, if any Include every person living on June 1, 1900. Omit children born since June 1, 1900.	Relationship of each person to the head of the family.
Street	Number	1	2	3	4

Census-taker's Form, 1900, enlarged section (b)

TWELFTH CENSUS OF THE UNITED STATES

SCHEDULE No. 1—POPULATION

of township, town, precinct, district, or other civil division, as the case may be. See Instructions.]

Name of Institution, – – –

above-named division,

me on the – – – – – – – – – – *day of June, 1900,* – – – – – – – – – – – – – – – – – –

PERSONAL DESCRIPTION								NATIVITY		
Color or race	Sex	DATE OF BIRTH		Age at last birthday	Whether single, married, widowed or divorced	Number of years married	Mother of how many children	Number of these children living	Place of birth of each person and parents of such person enumerated. If born in the United States, also the State or Territory; if of foreign birth, give the Country only		
		Month	Year						Place of birth of this Person	Place of birth of FATHER of this person	Place of birth of MOTHER of this person
5	6	7		8	9	10	11	12	13	14	15

Census-taker's Form, 1900, enlarged section (c)

Supervisor's District No. -------------- } *Sheet No.* --------------

Enumeration District No. --------------

Ward of city, --------------

-------------- *, Enumerator.*

CITIZENSHIP.		OCCUPATION, TRADE, OR PROFESSION of each person TEN years of age and over.		EDUCATION.				OWNERSHIP OF HOME			
Year of immigration to the United States	Number of years in the United States	OCCUPATION.	Months not employed	Attended school (in months)	Can read.	Can write.	Can speack English.	Owned or tended.	Owned free or mortgaged.	Farm or house.	Number of farm schedule.
	Naturalization										
16	17	19	20	21	22	23	24	25	26	27	28
	18										

1

2

3

Bibliography

Books

Alonso, William, and Paul Starr, eds. *The Politics of Numbers*. Washington, D.C.: Russell Sage Foundation, 1986.

Anderson, Margo J. *The American Census: A Social History*. New Haven, Conn.: Yale University Press, 1988.

Anderson, Margo J., and Stephen E. Fienberg. *Who Counts? The Politics of Census-Taking in Contemporary America*. Washington, D.C.: Russell Sage Foundation, 1999.

Barringer, Harbert R., Robert W. Gardner, and Michael J. Levin. *Asians and Pacific Islanders in the United States*. New York: Russell Sage Foundation, 1993.

Browning, Don S., et al. *From Culture Wars to Common Ground: Religion and the American Family*. Louisville, Ky.: Westminster/John Knox Press, 1997.

Canon, David T. *Race, Redistricting, and Representation: The Unintended Consequences of Black Majority Districts*. Chicago: University of Chicago Press, 1999.

Caplow, Theodore, Louis Hicks, and Ben J. Wattenberg. *The First Measured Century: An Illustrated Guide to Trends in America, 1900–2000*. Washington, D.C.: AEI Press, 2000.

Carlson, Richard C., and Bruce Goldman. *Fast Forward: Where Technology, Demographics, and History Will Take America and the World in the Next Thirty Years*. New York: HarperBusiness, 1994.

Choldin, Harvey M. *Looking for the Last Percent: The Controversy over Census Undercounts*. New Brunswick, N.J.: Rutgers University Press, 1994.

Cole, Thomas R. *The Journey of Life: A Cutural History of Aging in America*. Cambridge, U.K.: Cambridge University Press, 1992.

Dychtwald, Ken. *Age Power: How the 21st Century Will Be Ruled by the New Old*. New York: Jeremy P. Tarcher/Putnam, 1999.

Ehrlich, Paul R., and Anne H. Ehrlich. *The Population Explosion*. New York: Simon & Schuster, 1990.

Farrell, Betty. *Family: The Making of an Idea, an Institution, and a Controversy in American Culture*. Boulder, Colo.: Westview Press, 1999.

Gerald, Debra E., ed. *Federal Forecasters Conference, 2000: Papers and Proceedings*. Washington, D.C.: U.S. Department of Education, 2000.

Harkavy, Oscar. *Curbing Population Growth: An Insider's Perspective on the Population Movement*. New York: Plenum Press, 1995.

Heer, David M. *Immigration in America's Future: Social Science Findings and the Policy Debate*. Boulder, Colo.: Westview Press, 1996.

Isbister, John. *The Immigration Debate: Remaking America*. West Hartford, Conn.: Kumarian Press, 1996.

Jacobson, Matthew Frye. *Whiteness of a Different Color: European Immigrants and the Alchemy of Race*. Cambridge, MA: Harvard University Press, 1998.

Jacoby, Tamar. *Someone Else's House: America's Unfinished Struggle for Integration*. New York: Free Press, 1998.

Mason, Mary Ann, Arlene S. Skolnick, and Stephen D. Sugarman, eds. *All Our Families: New Policies for a New Century; A Report of the Berkeley Family Forum*. Oxford, U.K.: Oxford University Press, 1998.

Mills, Karen M. *Americans Overseas in U.S. Censuses*. Washington, DC: Bureau of the Census, 1993.

Narayan, Uma, and Julia J. Bartkowiak, eds. *Having and Raising Children: Unconventional Families, Hard Choices, and the Social Good*. University Park, Pa.: Pennsylvania State University Press, 1999.

Nobles, Melissa. *Shades of Citizenship: Race and the Census in Modern Politics*. Stanford, CA: Stanford University Press, 2000.

Peterson, Peter G. *Gray Dawn: How the Coming Age Wave Will Transform America—and the World*. New York: Times Books, 1999.

Raban, Jonathan. *Bad Land: An American Romance*. New York: Pantheon, 1996.

Risman, Barbara J. *Gender Vertigo: American Families in Transition*. New Haven, Conn.: Yale University Press, 1998.

Rodriguez, Clara E. *Changing Race: Latinos, the Census, and the History of Ethnicity in the United States*. New York: NYU Press, 2000.

Ryscavage, Paul. *Income Inequality in America: An Analysis of Trends*. Armonk, NY: M. E. Sharpe, 1998.

Skerry, Peter. *Counting on the Census? Race, Group Identity, and the Evasion of Politics*. Washington, D.C.: Brookings Institution Press, 2000.

Skocpol, Theda. *The Missing Middle: Working Families and the Future of American Social Policy*. New York: Norton, 2000.

Suro, Roberto. *Strangers Among Us: How Latino Immigration Is Transforming America*. New York: Knopf, 1998.

Sussman, Marvin B., Suzanne K. Steinmetz, and Gary W. Peterson, eds. *Handbook of Marriage and the Family*, 2nd ed. New York: Plenum Press, 1999.

Taylor, Robert Joseph, James S. Jackson, and Linda M. Chatters, eds. *Family Life in Black America*. Thousand Oaks, Calif.: Sage Publications, 1997.

U.S. Bureau of the Census. *The Handbook for a Better Census: Opportunities for Governors' Liaisons*. Washington, D.C.: U.S. Department of Commerce, Bureau of the Census, 1998.

———. *Census 2000 Complete Count Committee: Handbook for Local Governments*. Washington, D.C.: U.S. Department of Commerce, Bureau of the Census, 1998.

U.S. Census Monitoring Board. *Census 2000: A National Process Requires Local Focus; Report to Congress, 1 February 1999*. Washington, D.C.: U.S. Census Monitoring Board, 1999.

———. *Report to Congress, 1 April, 1999*. Washington, D.C.: U.S. Census Monitoring Board, 1999.

———. *Report to Congress, 1 February, 1999*. Washington D.C.: U.S. Census Monitoring Board, 1999.

Weiss, Jessica. *To Have and To Hold: Marriage, the Baby Boom, and Social Change*. Chicago: University of Chicago Press, 2000.

Web Site

www.census.gov

The official Web site of the Census Bureau, this site provides data from the most recent census as it is processed and released; demographic maps; and overview reports on particular topics, illustrated with charts and graphs; as well as information about the census itself, advice on using the statistics and on genealogical research, a catalog of publications by the Bureau, and two population clocks, for the U.S. and the world.

Additional Periodical Articles with Abstracts

More information on America's changing demography can be found in the following articles. Readers who require a more comprehensive selection are advised to consult *Readers Guide to Periodical Literature, Readers Guide Abstracts, Social Sciences Abstracts*, and other H.W. Wilson publications.

Hispanic Teens Set Urban Beat. Jeffery D. Zbar. *Advertising Age*, v. 72 pS6 June 25, 2001.

In the author's view, the 2000 census sent a clear message to U.S. marketers that the Hispanic population, and its youth in particular, cannot be ignored. According to Roberto Ramos, founder and president of upstart Hispanic youth marketing company Ruido Group, New York, Hispanic youths have only recently been recognized as an important market. Although some marketers are uncertain about how to communicate with this audience, a 2000 Hispanic–teens study conducted by Roslow Research Group says that advertising to Hispanics in Spanish is a lot more effective than advertising in English to bilingual Hispanics.

The End of Family? Terry Golway. *America*, v. 185 p6 July 16–23, 2001.

In Golway's opinion, the United States Census Bureau's numbers for 2000 have been used by the media to ratify the impressionistic, anecdotal conclusions that the traditional family is fading fast, but this may not be true. There has been an increase in the percentage of black children in two-parent households, and the same is true among Hispanic children. Seventy-five percent of white children live with two parents, a surprisingly high figure given all the hype in recent years. Golway concludes that people in the media seem to be exaggerating the end of the traditional American family. The media's reporting is filled with the bias of false inclusion, and anyone who insists that two parents are better than one is immediately dismissed as a right-wing fanatic who seeks to impose outdated ideas of morality and family on others. Golway finds something disturbing about the media's enthusiasm for nontraditional families.

Blowin' Smoke. Allison Stein Wellner. *American Demographics*, v. 23 pp20–21 February 2001.

Wellner discusses a new analysis by the Centers for Disease Control and Prevention (CDC) in Atlanta revealing that roughly half of the population, or 135 million people, have had some experience with cigarettes. The report notes that over 90 million people in the U.S. have smoked 100 cigarettes or more in their lives, and of this group, an estimated 45 million have given them up. There are 47 million current smokers in the U.S., according to CDC estimates, with male smokers slightly outnumbering female smokers. Before 1998, adults aged 25 to 44 were the most likely to smoke, but the biggest share of smokers today are aged between 18 and 24. Other statistics on smoking in the U.S. are discussed.

The Diversity Myth. William H. Frey. *American Demographics*, v. 20 pp38 43 June 1998.

Frey's analysis of the latest population estimates from the U.S. Census Bureau indicates that the much-hyped increase in ethnic and racial diversity is not a reality. Indeed, population shifts during the 1990s point to continued geographic concentration of minority groups into specific regions and a small number of metro areas. A detailed analysis of the available statistics on minority patterns is provided.

Mixed Doubles: Intermarriage. William H. Frey. *American Demographics*, v. 21 pp56–62 November 1999.

A recent analysis of U.S. Census Bureau data suggests that the numbers of interracial and interethnic marriages are increasing. The data show that the number of married couples who are of different races or ethnic groups has doubled since 1980 and that these couples tend to be young, upscale, and well-educated. Moreover, a computer analysis conducted by William H. Frey, senior fellow of demographic studies at the Milken Institute in Santa Monica and a professor at the State University of New York–Albany, using data from the Census Bureau's 1998 Current Population Survey, shows that the increase in the number of mixed marriages is eliminating, or at least changing, long-held barriers. The findings of Frey's analysis provide the first detailed insight into the scale and features of this phenomena, which may transform the U.S. family and the consumer marketplace in the long term. These findings are discussed in detail.

Recasting the Melting Pot. Roberto Suro. *American Demographics,* v. 21 pp30–32 March 1999.

What Suro calls "the myth of the melting pot" informs expectations for the first half of the next century, when another great wave of immigration is expected. Almost 50 percent of all immigrants come from Spanish-speaking countries, and the U.S. Census Bureau estimates that Latinos will account for over 40 percent of population growth in the next decade. In Suro's opinion, the melting-pot metaphor is not very helpful in understanding where this demographic change is taking America, however, and it may create false or misleading expectations as far as Latinos are concerned. How Latinos tend to assimilate themselves into the larger American community is discussed.

Second-Generation Question Mark: The Real Test Is How Immigrants' Children Will Do. Tamar Jacoby. *American Enterprise*, v. 11 pp32+ December 2000.

Jacoby notes that there are mixed views on how second-generation U.S. immigrants will fare in the future. She points out that many areas where immigrants settle have conditions that enforce racial and ethnic isolation and foster an outsider mentality. Where education is concerned, Hispanics have a number of problems, including high school-dropout rates and low-level college attendance, that are not shared by Asians and that may inhibit their entry into the mainstream. But she observes that Latino immigrants also have an array of strengths, such as high labor force participation rates, strong families, and industrious work habits. The fundamental criterion, in Jacoby's opinion, should be whether these young people are becoming more successful—and more "American"—than their parents. Although it is likely that some groups will join the mainstream more rapidly than others, optimists argue that many second-generation immigrants are achieving more than their parents ever thought possible, and that their future is not so bleak as once supposed.

The New Urban Demographics: Race, Space, and Boomer Aging. William H. Frey. *Brookings Review*, v. 18 pp20–23 Summer 2000.

In the author's view, the urban landscape of America is transforming. The familiar differences between the growing Sunbelt and the more sluggish Frostbelt areas of the country are being complicated by new demographic trends, in particular the sharp rise in immigration to America and the aging of the baby boomers. Every year, around one million people, mainly Latin American and Asian in origin, arrive in America, the majority settling in urban areas. This new immigration is infusing many urban areas with residents from a range of backgrounds and suggests the necessity for a new way of thinking about the demographic profiles of cities and suburbs. Meanwhile, most baby boomers, a large cohort of 76 million people, will not move as they get older but "age in place" in the suburbs rather than the city. Frey believes these trends are sure to complicate urban and suburban race-ethnic and aging demographic dynamics.

Pols Are Salivating Over Asian Americans. Alexandra Starr. *Business Week*, pp42–43 September 10, 2001.

Asian-Americans are the third-largest minority in the United States and are growing in numbers and concentration in key areas. The author reports that these 12 million people are teetering between the two parties, and that GOP leaders believe that the right combination of policy and politics could sway them toward the Republicans. Asians are not set to have as much political power as Latinos, who outnumber them three to one. More Asians are spreading out beyond Hawaii, California, and New York, however, and in almost 100 congressional districts they account for at least 5 percent of the population. Asian voting tendencies and the tactics of both parties to woo them as voters are examined.

An End to Counting by Race? Tamar Jacoby. *Commentary*, v. 111, pp37–40 June 2001.

As the author explains, the decennial census required by the U.S. Constitution has always been entangled with questions of race, but the one that reached the nation in March 2000 was different. On both versions of the questionnaire, a question listed more than one category for race, and, surprisingly, around 7 million Americans described themselves as more than just black, Asian, Latin, Korean, or any other category listed. The change in the 2000 census was the product of a long, bitter political battle that began in the early 1990s when a small group of interracial families started to lobby the government for their children's right to describe themselves as "multiracial" on the census. The author claims that the response to the 2000 census is not the first indication in American history or the modern world that human reality is too varied and fluid to be shoehorned into racial categories, nor is it the only sign that Americans are tired of rigid racial categories. The more Americans view ethnic and even racial identity as a matter of personal choice, the fuzzier such categories will grow and the harder it will be for governments to traffic in them.

In Asian America. Tamar Jacoby. *Commentary*, v. 110 pp21–28 July/August 2000.

Since the Immigration and Nationality Act was passed in 1965, the Asian-American community has been totally transformed. Although Asian-Americans are hugely diverse as a group, they are often perceived as a single entity by both themselves and other Americans, with their common unifying factor being their newness to the country. Between 60 and 70 percent of them are foreign-born, with the result that it is the growing second generation that will set the scene for the Asian-American experience. Although they are faced with the challenge of fitting in, they are doing so in an era of unprecedented affluence and at a time when the ideology of "diversity" makes it possible for them to decide if and how they will assimilate into American society. The writer discusses the self-imposed obstacles that lie in the way of assimilation.

Labor's Changing Accent. James B. Arndorfer. *Crain's Chicago Business*, v. 24, pp1+ June 25, 2001.

The author reports on the transformation Chicago is witnessing in the composition of its population. According to the 2000 census, the city's Hispanic population grew by 38 percent to 735,644 between 1990 and 2000. This represents one out of every four Chicagoans. Ric Gudell, director of vocation trade school at the Chicago Manufacturing Institute, says that Hispanic laborers now make up as much as 40 percent of the 620,000 manufacturing jobs in Chicago and its suburbs. In response, manufacturing companies are recruiting bilingual supervisors and implementing education programs aimed at Hispanic employees. Hispanic-oriented community groups are also launching training programs, in an effort to help people move from service-sector jobs to better-paying factory work. Experts believe that Chicago's ability to compete in manufacturing depends on the successful integration of this growing segment of the local workforce.

Race and Ethnicity and the Controversy over the U.S. Census. Margo Anderson and Stephen E. Fienberg. *Current Sociology*, v. 48 pp87–110 July 2000.

Race and ethnicity in relation to the controversy over the 2000 census in the U.S. is discussed. The authors note that at the 1990 census, a coalition of city and state governments sued the Census Bureau before the count, claiming that even before the census took place they knew that it would be affected by an undercount. The history of this lawsuit and the planning for the 2000 census controversies are examined. It is pointed out that the 2000 census is controversial because of a plan to correct the census counts for the undercount of blacks and other minorities, using the results of a sample taken after the completion of the regular count, and because of a new format for the question on race that permits respondents to identify with more than one racial group. The technical data and methods behind such controversies, the racial and ethnic categories that underlie the undercount controversy, and the process leading up to the new racial and ethnic categories being used in the 2000 census are explored.

The Golden State Turns Brown: Census Reveals No Racial or Ethnic Majority in California. *Economist*, v. 359 p36 April 7, 2001.

According to the 2000 census, the number of Californians who describe themselves as white has fallen behind the number who describe themselves as something else since the census taken in 1990. The change has been quick: The drop in the number of whites since the 1950s is steep and is accelerating. The *Economist* believes that, in taking this path, California is revealing to the rest of the U.S. its future—one in which whites and blacks will share the nation with a larger proportion of the population that has Asian or Latin American origins. However, rather than having an adverse effect on the nature of the U.S., immigrants to the country will continue to become American as they mildly change the American mixture. Immigrants to California tend to be Hispanic and Asian, and this fact will continue to shape the character of the state, but it will not change its Americanness. The real challenge in California's census figures comes not from the fine print but from the simplest figure of all—the state's population grand total: 33.9 million people and growing quickly.

Primary Colours: New Census Figures on Race and Ethnicity. *Economist*, v. 358 pp27–28 March 17, 2001.

Statistics relating to race from the 2000 census, which were released in March 2001 by the Census Bureau, indicate that every racial or ethnic group in the U.S., including the white majority, is getting bigger. Of the 281.4 million people within the borders of the U.S., some 211 million stated that they are white. This is an increase of 12 million from the previous census figures, but a slightly lower share of the total. As a result of immigration and higher birth rates, the white share of the population is dipping as other groups grow faster. The population of Latinos has grown the most and, for the first time, this group is roughly as large as the black total. Blacks have responded by arguing that the growth in numbers of Latinos is explained by a re-ordering of questions on the census form that places the Latino choice higher up. The black population also recorded a significant rise in numbers, partly as a result of a campaign by minority groups to persuade more people to send back their census forms. The Census Bureau contends that there will be an increase in the proportion of mixed-race people in the U.S. in the future.

Sun, Sun, Sun, and Idaho. *Economist*, v. 358 pp26–7 January 6, 2001.

Preliminary results from the 2000 U.S. census confirm a trend that has shown up since 1945: the population is still shifting away from the industrial North toward the Sunbelt states of the South and West. The gravitational pull of the Sunbelt is nothing new, but the 2000 census data reveal that the strongest growth is no longer in California and Florida. William Frey, a demographer at the University of Michigan, argues that a "new Sunbelt" has emerged that relies on the opportunities of high technology to attract young professionals inward from the east and west coasts. One of the largest winners in the 2000 census was Texas, which Frey argues represents both the old and new Sunbelts. In recent years it has seen an influx both of young workers to fill technology jobs and immigrants coming north from Latin America. Given that more people bring more power, Republicans are salivating over the 2000 census data. The concentration of newcomers in sunny and mountainous regions means that states won by George W. Bush will pick up seven congressional seats and seven electoral college votes. The high political stakes riding on the census are discussed.

Every Single Nose. Eileen Shanahan. *Governing*, v. 12 pp32+ September 1999.

Shanahan reports that countless ideas are emerging in order to increase awareness about the 2000 Census and ensure that states are not disadvantaged, financially and politically, by inaccurate numbers. Adverse factors, such as mistrust of government, transient lifestyles, and an increase in junk mail, have heightened fears that many will not fill out their census applications. As a result, states, local governments, and volunteers have had to make huge efforts to ensure the maximum count. Every single residence must be located, even those in trailer parks, nursing homes, and other areas where residents have no fixed address. Coupled with these efforts is a huge motivational drive to encourage people to fill out and return their census forms. These measures, among others, are designed to ensure that the count will be as accurate and cost-effective as possible.

Election 2000 and the Culture War. Jeffrey S. Victor. *Humanist*, v. 61 pp5–7 January/February 2001.

The author argues that the presidential election of 2000 reflects a growing "culture war" in American society. According to some political commentators, the results of the election reveal that American citizens have altered the way in which they usually vote and that voters' judgments are now based on individual moral beliefs rather than on group affinities, such as socioeconomic status, ethnicity, gender, region, and urban-rural residence. Moral beliefs have always collectively reflected the social influence of people's group connections, however, and these connections still influence which side a person takes in the internal conflicts of American culture. The writer discusses exit poll data from the 2000 presidential election indicating the influence of rural-urban, ethnic, and gender differences upon the vote, as well as differences in religious belief and socioeconomic position.

Laconia, Indiana: Population 29. Evan West. *Indianapolis Monthly*, v. 24 p114–119+ August 2001.

The author considers Laconia, Indiana, as a symbol of fading, small-town Americana. This spring, the town's residents found themselves in the national spotlight when the early 2000 census results were released. The Associated

Press ran a story about the disappearance of small-town America and chose Laconia from the thousands of towns whose population dropped during the last decade of the 20th century. The census indicates that Laconia had a population of 75 in 1990 and 29 in 2000, but residents do not believe the numbers tell the true story or that they are even correct. The town was once a thriving settlement, but after its school closed in the 1950s, things started to decline, as children were pulled from the community, eliminating an important symbol of independence, continuity, and pride. The battle to save Laconia is discussed.

How Census Results Could Redefine America's Definition of Black. *Jet,* v. 99 pp4–10 April 2, 2001.

The 2000 Census marked the first time respondents could check more than one race. Nearly 7 million Americans took advantage of the option, and of these, nearly 2 million African-Americans said they belonged to more than one race. Taking all variations into account, there were 63 different ways in which the race question could be answered, which is in stark contrast to the five racial categories on the 1990 Census form. Although conflict between what race people believe themselves to be and what race society chooses to label them as will likely continue, in *Jet*'s opinion the Census results have gone far in redefining America's definition of black. The magazine reports that many have praised the Census for taking a progressive approach to the race issue, but some have been critical of the bureau for not finding a clear way to interpret the numbers gathered.

Get Ready to Use Census 2000 Data. John Kavaliunas. *Marketing Research*, v. 12 pp42–43 Fall 2000.

The author mentions that the U.S. Census Bureau will release the first results from Census 2000 before December 31, 2000, when it sends the apportionment counts to the president. These counts will provide statistics on the number of persons by state, together with an indication of the number of seats each state has an entitlement to in the House of Representatives. The data will be available in many different types and formats, first on the Internet and later on CD-ROM and DVD. In order to use the data effectively, it is necessary to understand how the different levels of statistical and political geography combine into an overall hierarchy, and which products contain pertinent information. A guide to understanding census geography and a timetable of what census data to expect and when are provided.

Stories of Self Definition. Clara E. Rodriguez. *NACLA Report on the Americas*, v. 34 pp41+ May/June 2001.

In these excerpts from the book *Changing Race*, Latinos who checked "other race" on a census form explain their choices.

Census Short-Count: Supreme Court Decision on Sampling. *The Nation*, v. 268 p3 February 15, 1999.

In *The Nation*'s view, the Supreme Court recently decided to permit the GOP to disenfranchise many poor and urban citizens when carrying out the 2000 census. The ostensible issue before the Court was whether to give the Census Bureau the power to employ sampling techniques to compensate for under-counting. *The Nation* argues that the decision will result in a still-larger con-centration of power in the hands of America's white, rich, and rural citizens at the expense of its nonwhite, poor, and urban ones.

Prisoner Nation. Beverly Gage. *The Nation*, v. 271 pp5–6 July 17, 2000.

The author argues that the prison boom will result in a skewed census result. According to anticipated census figures, because prisoners are counted as res-idents of the towns where they are serving time, hundreds of thousands of blacks and Latinos are regarded as living in rural communities, and they will be followed by government funding and voting clout. With around 2 million people imprisoned nationwide, this census technicality will result in a multi-billion-dollar boon for the rural towns that accommodate most of the country's prisoners. Moreover, prisoners skew communities' income statistics down-ward, making prison towns prime candidates for poverty-directed dollars. Like many other byproducts of the prison boom, the skewed count will badly affect the inner city, which loses federal funds and voting power with every inmate who is taken away.

Don't Box Me In: Census Needs to Drop Racial Checkoffs. Ward Con-nerly. *National Review*, v. 53 pp24–26 April 16, 2001.

Connerly suggests that the time has come for America to renounce race classi-fications. Getting the government out of the business of classifying its people and asking them to check the ridiculous little race boxes represents the next step in America's long journey toward becoming one nation. It will help free Americans from the expensive and poisonous identity politics that define their political process. It will also clip the wings of a government that has become so intrusive that it classifies its citizens on the basis of race, even when respon-dents "decline to state." The writer describes how he is preparing to place a Racial Privacy Initiative before California voters on the 2002 ballot that would bar governments in California from classifying individuals by race, color, eth-nicity, or national origin.

Minority Report: Hispanics. *National Review*, v. 53 pp15–18 April 2, 2001.

The 2000 census shows that Hispanics have drawn almost level with blacks as an American minority. In 1990, there were 30 million blacks in the United States and 22.4 million Hispanics; now there are 36.4 million blacks and 35.3 million Hispanics. The consequences of this shift for America's future are pro-found, in the writer's opinion; even if the numbers hold steady, there will be a shift in the emphasis Americans place on particular historical events. How-ever, those people linked by the term Hispanic do not have much in common with each other, and assimilation may make them more or less distinct. The writer also discusses why immigration should be restricted.

As Diversity Sweeps Nation, a Placid Town Is Unchanged. Dan Barry. *New York Times*, pA1 May 4, 2001.

Despite the population shifts and racial diversity reflected in the latest census, there are still communities like Selinsgrove, Pa., where the population remains constant and almost entirely white. The article examines this phenonema and the race relations between the citizens of Selinsgrove and the few minority members of the community.

As Others Abandon Plains, Indians and Bison Come Back. Timothy Egan. *New York Times*, p1 May 27, 2001.

Egan reports that, according to the most recent census, previously all-white areas of America's Great Plains are emptying out. At the same time, American Indians are moving back in.

Blacks Split on Disclosing Multiracial Roots. Eric Schmitt. *New York Times*, p1 March 31, 2001.

According to U.S. Census figures, the black community is divided over the use of the recently-introduced multiracial category. Vicksburg, Miss., and Lawton, Okla., are two places with thriving black communities that underscore how much racial identity is influenced by segregation and oppression, levels of integration and local history. In interviews, residents discuss their reasons for using, or not using, the multiracial category.

Census Fight Is Put on Hold Until a Count Is Completed. Steven A. Holmes. *New York Times*, p34 October 31, 1999.

Holmes reports that, following three years of partisan bickering over the census, Democrats and Republicans have called a halt to the battle over whether the Census Bureau can use statistical sampling to supplement the next census. They have decided to wait until after the census is completed next year to determine whether population figures derived from sampling—interviewing residents from a sample of 300,000 households—can be used to draw boundaries for Congressional and state legislative districts.

New Suburbs, New Alignments: Demographic Shifts Reflected in Census Figures. Op-ed. William H. Frey. *New York Times*, pA23 March 24, 1998.

Recent census figures suggest that cities may have more in common with their surrounding suburbs than they do with cities in other regions of the country. Suburbs and cities are losing their middle-class residents, who are being replaced with new immigrants. The author believes that eventually the country could split into old metropolitan areas that are increasingly multiethnic and white-dominated population centers, mainly in the Southeast and Rocky Mountain West.

The New U.S.: Grayer and More Hispanic; Census Bureau Report. Katharine Q. Seelye. *New York Times*, pB16 March 27, 1997.

A new report by the Census Bureau projects that by the year 2005 Hispanic Americans will surpass blacks as the nation's largest minority and by 2050 will account for one-fourth of the U.S. population. The report, "Demographic State of the Nation," also projects that by 2028, the number of white Americans who die will exceed the number of those being born.

Politics and the Census: Supreme Court Rules Against Sampling. Robert J. Samuelson. *Newsweek*, v. 133 p48 February 8, 1999.

Just before April 1, 2000, the Census Bureau will attempt to count everyone in the United States. Samuelson predicts this bid will fail as it always has and will in the future. He discusses the Clinton administration's proposed use of statistical sampling instead of a traditional head count and explains why he believes that such a move would threaten the integrity of a system that has until now enjoyed public confidence.

Unmarried, with Children. Barbara Kantrowitz and Pat Wingert. *Newsweek*, v. 137 pp46–54 May 28, 2001.

The authors report on the current condition of the American family. Recently released figures from the 2000 Census reveal that the number of families headed by single mothers has risen 25 percent since 1990. Contributing to this figure are a high rate of divorce and out-of-wedlock births, and demographers now estimate that over 50 percent of children born in the 1990s will spend at least part of their childhood in a single-parent home. This new breed of single mother could be any age and any race, she may be divorced or never married, and she may be a single mother by choice or cohabiting with a man who may be the father of one or more of her children. Many women would rather stay single if they cannot find the perfect soulmate, and some are the adult children of divorce who want to avoid putting their own children through the pain of watching a parent leave. The implications for children belonging to single-parent families are discussed.

Immigration, Domestic Migration, and Demographic Balkanization in America: New Evidence for the 1990s. William H. Frey. *Population and Development Review*, v. 22 pp741–763 December 1996.

Frey argues that the recent scrutiny given to the impact of post-1965 immigration to the United States has largely overlooked an important long-term consequence: social and demographic divisions, across regions, that are being created by distinctly different migration patterns of immigrants and domestic, mostly native-born, migrants. Evidence for 1990–95 shows a continuation of highly focused destinations among immigrants whose race-ethnic and skill-level profiles differ from those of the rest of the population; migration patterns among domestic migrants favoring areas that are not attracting immigrants; and accentuated domestic outmigration away from high immigration areas that is most evident for less educated and lower-income long-term residents. These separate migration patterns are leading to widening divisions by race-ethnicity and population growth across broad regions of the country. These patterns are likely to make immigrant assimilation more difficult and social and political cleavages more pronounced.

First Glimpses from the 2000 U.S. Census. Mary M. Kent, Kelvin M. Pollard, and John Haaga. *Population Bulletin*. v. 56 pp1–39 June 2001.

The first findings from the 2000 U.S. census are presented and examined. Topics discussed include the census tradition; population change; increase in the number of Hispanics within the population; racial and ethnic diversity; metropolitan growth; political implications of the census findings; media coverage of the census; selected data to be released from the census; the legacy of the 2000 census; and the next census.

Are the Children of Today's Immigrants Making It? Joel Perlmann and Roger Waldinger. *Public Interest*, pp73–96 Summer 1998.

The authors point out that the children of today's immigrants must perform well and early if they are to advance in American society. This is due to the fact that the recent restructuring of the American economy allows them no time to play catch-up. Nonetheless, a study of previous immigration to America indicates that, overall, the children of post-1965 immigrants start life with disadvantages that are no greater than those faced by immigrant children before. The history of the experiences of immigrants to the United States is outlined.

Multiracials, Intermarriage, Ethnicity: U.S. Census. Joel Perlmann. *Society,* v. 34 pp30–23 September/October 1997.

Perlmann explains that deciding how the census in the year 2000 should handle the issue of multiracial people is currently an issue of contention. In Perlmann's analysis, this has become the case because a decision is needed soon, because multiracial people have found a voice, and because the decision might affect race-based laws and politics. In particular, many people concerned with civil rights or with the power of racial minorities do not want to add complexities to the struggle for racial equality. Similarly, the future racial composition of the United States is a major issue; telling Americans that their country will be more than half nonwhite by the middle of the 21st century stimulates different reactions. Some believe that the demographic projection says America had better wake up to the needs of its minorities who are soon to become its majority; others believe the projection says America had better restrict immigration to avoid reaching a nonwhite majority.

Small Town, Mass Society, and the 21st Century. James Wright. *Society,* v. 38 pp3–10 November/December 2000.

Although the Census regularly shows increased urbanization in the United States, the populations of most of the truly large American cities have been decreasing for decades. Seven of the nation's ten largest cities as of 1970 were noticeably smaller in 1990, a pattern that continued into the last decade of the 20th century. In the author's view, the small-town presence in modern American life appears to be more powerful than at any time in the past 50 years; he notes that between 1990 and 1996 the fastest-growing American city was actually Henderson, Nevada. In addition to the recent escalation in the popularity of such small-town staples as country and western music, stock car racing, and traditional Christian religiosity, he observes that many products are now marketed to appeal to small-town sentimentality.

An Amazing Journey. Roger Simon and Angie Cannon. *U.S. News and World Report*, v. 131 pp10–18 August 6, 2001.

The similarities and differences between the United States of 100 years ago and the U.S. of today are discussed, in part by comparing a family living in a New York tenement in 1900 with the people who live there now. The picture that emerges from this *U.S. News* study is that of a country defined by the immigrant experience, even though today's immigrants come from very different places. In the course of the century, America has become more diverse. Nowadays the majority of the population can be found in metropolitan areas. Far more people own their own homes, but families are smaller, people put off having children or getting married, and more people simply live together. The number of single parents is increasing, and millions live alone. Salaries, education, health, life expectancy, and working conditions have improved.

A Nation of New Cities: Census Shows Effect of Immigration on Growth of Cities. Angie Cannon, Kit R. Roane, and Stephen Sawicki. *U.S. News and World Report*, v. 130 pp16–18 April 2, 2001.

According to figures from the U.S. Census Bureau, immigrants are helping to halt the population drain from several major urban centers and making those cities and inner suburbs increasingly diverse, and in some instances slightly less segregated. The trend may continue on a grander scale in years to come. Cities that did not receive an influx of immigrants often lost population, revenue, and political clout as middle-class people moved out and were not replaced. Various cities are compared.

Advertisers Are Cautious as Household Makeup Shifts. Vanessa O'Connell and Jon E. Hilsenrath. *Wall Street Journal* (eastern edition), ppB1+ May 15, 2001.

New census data to be released today (May 15) shows only 23.5% of 2000 households were traditional families. The authors report that marketers are targeting the huge numbers of single mothers, unmarried couples and others with caution, so as not to seem condescending.

Exploring a Nation of Extremes. Nicholas Kulish, Kelly Greene, and Will Pinkston. *Wall Street Journal* (eastern edition), ppB1+ May 25, 2001.

The 2000 U.S. census data breaks household data down to the county level. Its county-by-county profile provides the answers to many demographic and geographic questions. It has found many ordinary places with extraordinary statistics as it explores a nation of extremes.

Marketers Tweak Strategies as Age Groups Realign. Lisa Vickery, Kelly Greene, and Shelly Branch. *Wall Street Journal* (eastern edition), ppB1+ May 15, 2001.

Additional data from the 2000 census released today (May 15) show a rise in people aged 35 to 54, fewer young adults, and more free-spending teen and preteen youngsters. The authors report that marketers are adjusting their strategies to profit from these age-group shifts.

Since Census Counts Convicts, Some Towns Can't Get Enough. Nicholas Kulish. *Wall Street Journal* (eastern edition), ppA1+ August 9, 2001.

The writer describes the municipality of Florence, Ariz., which has profitably discovered that the Census Bureau counts prison inmates the same as law-abiding citizens, and has added 11,830 prisoners in several facilities located within its limits. The town's regular population of 5,224 has benefited from new parks, town offices, community and senior centers, and new police and fire facilities under construction. Due to Florence's outsized share of prisoners, millions of extra dollars in state and federal funding pour into its coffers annually, with an additional $1.76 from state and federal allocations based strictly on its prison population for every dollar generated by local taxes and fees.

Why the Census of 2000 Failed to Count Arabs. Nicholas Kulish. *Wall Street Journal* (eastern edition), ppB1+ September 26, 2001.

Kulish reports that there are few reliable estimates of how many Arabs or Muslims there are in the U.S. because the 2000 Census did not have a single category for people of Middle Eastern descent or for Muslims. The Census Bureau said that federal guidelines did not mandate an Arab category and that respondents are not asked for religious affiliation at all.

The Census Snarl. *Wilson Quarterly*, v. 21 pp115–116 Autumn 1997.

The 2000 census is a source of controversy. Everybody concerned with it appears to prize scientific accuracy, but, for the most part, only selectively. The writer reviews articles on the topic, covering the debates over the proposal to make a statistical adjustment to the head count to adjust for the predictable failure to reach all black Americans and other minorities, the proposal to add a multiracial category to more accurately reflect the condition of persons of mixed ancestry, and the proposal to delete all classifications founded on the unscientific idea of race.

Index